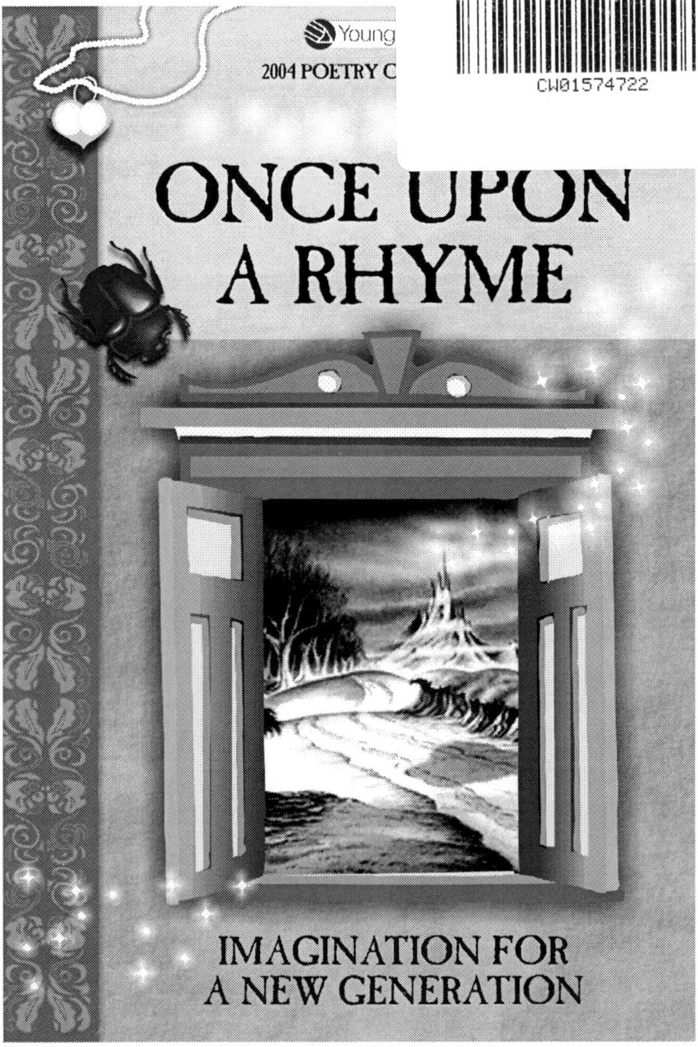

Northern Essex

Edited by Steve Twelvetree

YoungWriters
First published in Great Britain in 2004 by:
Young Writers
Remus House
Coltsfoot Drive
Peterborough
PE2 9JX
Telephone: 01733 890066
Website: www.youngwriters.co.uk

SB ISBN 1 84460 514 0

Foreword

Young Writers was established in 1991 and has been passionately devoted to the promotion of reading and writing in children and young adults ever since. The quest continues today. Young Writers remains as committed to engendering the fostering of burgeoning poetic and literary talent as ever.

This year's Young Writers competition has proven as vibrant and dynamic as ever and we are delighted to present a showcase of the best poetry from across the UK. Each poem has been carefully selected from a wealth of *Once Upon A Rhyme* entries before ultimately being published in this, our twelfth primary school poetry series.

Once again, we have been supremely impressed by the overall high quality of the entries we have received. The imagination, energy and creativity which has gone into each young writer's entry made choosing the best poems a challenging and often difficult but ultimately hugely rewarding task - the general high standard of the work submitted amply vindicating this opportunity to bring their poetry to a larger appreciative audience.

We sincerely hope you are pleased with our final selection and that you will enjoy *Once Upon A Rhyme Northern Essex* for many years to come.

Contents

St Margaret's CE Primary School, Halstead

St Peter's CE Primary School, Sible Hedingham

Stanway Primary School

The Poems

Highland Haikus

The loch is sleeping,
Moving, swaying peacefully,
Fish swim through the reeds.

Waterfalls crashing,
Glittering in the sunlight,
Echoing through caves.

Cattle are eating,
Munching the grass peacefully,
Moving quietly.

Birds fly gracefully,
Gliding through the sky high up,
Enjoying the view.

Ben Lait (10)
Boxted CE Primary School

Highland Haikus

Cattle are sleeping,
Lying very peacefully,
Then they awaken.

Mountains lay rocky,
Silent, bumpy and grassy
And wait for the rain.

The river runs wild,
It hits the side with a crash,
Very cold and wet.

The cliff edge drops far,
You see the lovely landscape,
It is beautiful.

Ben Maguire (9)
Boxted CE Primary School

Highland Haikus

Woodlands far away,
Cliff top, mountain top greenlands,
Waterfalls falling.

Rivers flowing fast,
Boats flowing very softly,
Heading for the caves.

Highland animals
Run along the mountain top,
Deer, cattle and sheep.

Shops scattered round town,
One road through, few cars are seen,
Where's all the people?

Matthew Wills (8)
Boxted CE Primary School

Highland Haikus

Strong winds smashing homes,
Stoney houses near the roads,
Dots of white houses.

Boats on the seashore,
Fishermen fishing for fish,
Tangled fishing nets.

Sloping hills so green,
Rocky mountains reaching high,
Water gently flows.

George Smith (9)
Boxted CE Primary School

Highland Haikus

See highland cattle
Strolling down the grassy slopes,
Eating lush green grass.

Waterfalls tumbling,
Smashing water on the rocks,
Splashing in the stream.

Golden sand glowing,
Seashells dotted on the bay,
Happy children play.

Deserted pathways,
Lurking trees sway in the wind,
The odd cars drive by.

Dark, spooky tunnels,
Spirits rise and protect them,
Forbidden entrance.

Alex MacPhail (10)
Boxted CE Primary School

The Tiger

A sneaker creeper,
A stalker walker,
A pouncer bouncer,
A tree climber,
A zebra finder,
A running hunter,
A striped character,
A tiger!

Lily Corrigan (10)
Boxted CE Primary School

Sunset

Sunset

Looking
At the pink clouds,
The red sun fades away,
Whispering clouds dance with the breeze,
Sunset.

Midnight

Shh! Shh!
Look at the stars,
Hear the howling wolf cry,
Watching the moon smile at the world,
Midnight.

Early morning

Tweet, tweet,
The swallow chirps,
The moon hides with the stars,
The sun gently lights the lead-black skies.
Morning.

Katie Weekes (10)
Boxted CE Primary School

Haunted House

A ghost lair,
A spider fair,
A child trapper,
A floorboard tapper,
A curtain shaker,
A bat baker,
A time taker,
A shadow maker.

Elizabeth Davies (9)
Boxted CE Primary School

Highland

Birds flying swiftly,
Swooping in the sky up high,
Rest in their nest.

Pebbles everywhere,
All over the sandy beach,
Smoothened by the sea.

Beautiful deer roam,
Dotted upon the cliff tops
Cantering gently.

Rivers flowing quietly,
Trickling around the mountains,
Silent as the night.

Maddie Weekes (10)
Boxted CE Primary School

Winter In The Playground

The playground is a white glimmering blanket of snow,
With footprints engraved in it.
People running
And smashing the transparent, protective pieces of plastic
That lie on the top of the puddles.

The playground is a war arena,
With bullets being fired,
And people getting shot,
People's bodies turning white,
Then there is a peace settlement
And the playground is deserted.

Adele Whatley (11)
Copford CE Primary School

The Goldilocks' Bear Rap

In a big, dark wood
not far away
three little bears
had porridge one day.

They saw it was hot
so they went for a walk
and there at the door
Goldilocks stalked.

She saw the porridge
and sat at the table
she tried them all
but liked Baby's porridge.

She ate it up
then sat on a chair
but broke it and said,
'Oh dear!'

She went upstairs
to have a nap
Dad's and Mum's
were very hard
but Baby Bear's
was just nice and soft.

When the bears came home
they saw the porridge,
they saw the chairs,
they saw the beds,
but when they saw Goldilocks . . .

They chased her out of the house.
When she thought she was safe
she got eaten by a lion!

Jacob Roberts (10)
Copford CE Primary School

The Goldilocks Rap

Deep in the wood
there lived three bears
and a girl
who did not care.
The bears ate porridge
and they went for a walk.
On their way out
they had a talk.

As they went
she gave a beat,
she ran in the house
to take a seat.

She tried the porridge,
one by one.
She tried them all
but liked Baby's one.

She sat on some seats
but they hurt her bum,
she broke Baby's seat
and thought she was dumb.

She went to the beds
and slept and slept.
When the bears came home,
they thought she was dead!

She jumped out the window
to run as fast as she can.
They called her back,
but she ran and ran!

Antonia Reason (10)
Copford CE Primary School

Little Gold Rap

In a deep, dark wood
Where no one goes,
Is a little girl
With curly bows.

She loves her porridge
She loves to rap,
She will wear anything
Apart from a cap.

Before she went,
She put on a hood
To go in the
Deep, dark wood.

She saw some porridge,
And ran to the chairs,
But before she sat down
She saw some hares.

She gobbled down the porridge
Then saw Baby's chair
She sat down, then
Snap went Baby's chair!

She was so surprised
She went to bed,
But when she woke up
She saw three heads.

She was tied to a chair
And pelted with porridge,
She was forced to open her mouth
To catch the dreadful porridge!

Joseph Abrehart-Briggs (9)
Copford CE Primary School

The Three Bears' Rap

Digging deep into the wood
Is a cottage with three bears.
There's a daddy bear, a baby bear
And a mummy bear who cares.

Mummy Bear, she cooks lots of porridge
That often is too hot,
So off they went for a walk
While the porridge cooled in the pot.

When they went they left the door
At a tilt with a big goodbye,
Then in came Goldie
With a great big sigh.

She tried some porridge
And took a bite,
She liked Baby Bear's
Because it was just right.

She sat on a chair
But it did not fit
She sat on Baby's
But she broke it!

She slept in a bed
Then turned on the light,
She saw three bears
And screamed with fright.

Chloe Hall (10)
Copford CE Primary School

Little Gold Rap

Deep in the woods
there lived three bears
Baby, Mummy and
Daddy Bear.

Mummy cooked some grub
put it in three bowls
they went for a walk
so Goldilocks strolled.

She ate Daddy's porridge,
but it was so grumpy,
the next one she tried
it was so lumpy,
she ate the third
because it was so lovely.

She sat on two chairs,
but they were so uncomfortable,
the last one she sat on
it went to a bumble.

She went upstairs
to have a snooze,
but when the bears came
she fell on her shoes.

Maisie Goldney (9)
Copford CE Primary School

The Autumn Leaves

I dreamt I saw a leaf,
It was all red and shiny,
I could not believe my eyes,
It was so beautiful and tiny.

As I trampled through the fallen leaves
I looked down to the ground,
I saw all the different coloured leaves
And then I heard a rustling sound.

It was a hedgehog snuffling for food,
To see what he could find.
Something small but very tasty,
Was on his hungry mind.

As the time moves on,
The trees are all bare.
All the leaves have fallen
In the windy autumn air.

Evelyn Thatcher (8)
Copford CE Primary School

Ode To A Snowball

Born from the snow in the neighbour's gutter,
You are the tight one, the cold one.
Soaring through the air in a gleaming arc,
Past the icicles, the frozen windows,
Until *splat!* You land on that ugly thing,
Known as . . . my sister's nose!

Laurence Knowles (11)
Dame Johane Bradbury's School

Invisible Beauty

She blows a gentle kiss to the small distressed and terrified leaves
that have fallen free.
The leaves go on their way, no longer scared, but happy
and ready for the new life ahead of them.

She is the beauty of the earth
the movement of the sea,
the direction of the fire.

When she is happy she wraps her cool, refreshing blanket
around the hot and tired worker.
She makes the water calm for the swan to land
and the children go for the swim they need.

When she is angry she swirls and swirls in an angry dance
leaving the houses and trees crumpled and sad.

But soon she calms with the sound of the rustling leaves.

William Andrews (11)
Dame Johane Bradbury's School

The Lake

Silent and still in the moonlight
The moon making it glow.
Shivering and rippling in the moonlight
As the wind whispers and blows.

Silent and still in the moonlight
As it peacefully lay.
Suddenly a splash!
A huge wave of water
As three children jump in to play.

Laughing, shrieking and beaming with joy
They all ran away and left with their noise,
At last as it peacefully lay
Silent and still in the moonlight.
It sleeps again.

May Crick (11)
Dame Johane Bradbury's School

Waterloo

As the muskets fire and the cannon reloads
The ranks of darkness charge again
The soldier aims
He aims and fires
And the coldest of lead strikes another man down.

As the muskets fire and the cannon reloads
The many troops charge, the many troops charge
And most of Europe rely on those men
Who fight for their lives, who fight for their honour
And who fight for their country
They fight with nothing but everything they have got
Yet the ranks of darkness charge again and again.

As the muskets fire and the cannon reloads
The Captain hoarsely yells his orders
With nothing but his duty and his honour
He shows determination in those dark eyes of blue
No forgiveness in that steely glare
And no mercy as he strikes another man down
Yet the ranks of darkness charge again and again,
How can this terror be stopped?

As the muskets fire and the cannon reloads
The ranks of darkness stand firm
The soldiers fight, they stand and fight
But the ranks of darkness hold firm.
And more soldiers charge, they never give up
And more fall, but more stand and fight
The ranks of darkness begin to fall.
The ranks of darkness are eventually defeated.

No muskets fire and no cannon reloads
As the saviours of their countries return home.
Many have fallen, but none have fled
And France was defeated at the battle of Waterloo.

Oliver Cairns (10)
Dame Johane Bradbury's School

The Candle And The Match

Light danced at the top of the world,
Chased by the dark,
Safe in its white world,
Till listen, hark.

A roaring of anger,
Evil, bloodshed, hate,
Evil wrenches open iron,
And springs from Satan's gate.

Black hooves, black manes,
A black cloak swept the world,
Light screams and runs,
No white held.

The dark is too quick,
It tramples the light,
The world is full of shadow,
No hope is in sight.

But the candle is provided,
And the match in our hands,
It's up to us to strike the light,
And whither Satan's bands.

Whether we be young or old,
This war is ours to fight,
No one else can save us,
It's up to us to find the light.

Emma Murray (11)
Dame Johane Bradbury's School

Penelope Plump

There once lived a girl called Penelope Plump,
Who lived in the local garbage dump.
She was very smelly but she had no belly,
For she hadn't been eating for weeks.
Nobody knew she even lived there
And they probably didn't want to look or stare.
She didn't even wear anything on her toes,
So if you go there hold your nose.
Now you know about Penelope Plump
Who lived in the local garbage dump.

Georgia Atkins (10)
East Bergholt CE (VC) Primary School

Spring

Honeybees flying
Pink, sweet fragranced roses
Soft, tiny, delicate violets
Prancing lambs and fluffy ducklings
Snowdrops creep upwards
Sparkling stars, glittering in the sky
I love spring.

Caitlin Leydon (10)
East Bergholt CE (VC) Primary School

The Thunderstorm

Lightning flashes as quick as a jaguar, darting through the sky.
Thunder like a scary tantrum, listen can you hear it cry?
Fierce waves crashing, foaming against the ever tall cliffs.
Swirling, strong winds picking up litter in enormous drifts.
But the lighthouse light still shines as strong as ever
In this dangerous and frightening weather.

Holly Clarke (9)
East Bergholt CE (VC) Primary School

Starry Night

Sun, sun, shining bright,
you have got all the light.
I wake up in the morning
and my mum and dad are snoring.
I open up my curtain,
and I am certain,
you will be there
and you will care.
Slowly then you start to set
lower in the sky you get.
I watch you get out of sight
darkness falls and it is night.

Star, star, in the night,
twinkle, twinkle, what a sight.
In my dreams you are calling
'Catch me gently I am falling,
keep me safely in your pocket,
in your heart and in your locket.
I will grant your wishes true
always happy, never blue.'
Then I wake with a cheerful heart
ready for the day to start.
The sky is blue, no sight of rain
the sun is coming up again.

Lydia Rose Eagle (9)
East Bergholt CE (VC) Primary School

The Day My Grandad Died

The day my grandad died was a sad day.
It was a mean day.
It was a horrible day.
It felt like a part of me had gone.
It felt like we weren't a proper family.
It was like the world had gone wrong.
It felt like we had done something wrong.

James Willing (10)
East Bergholt CE (VC) Primary School

A Season's Gift

When the sun rises I feel a shiver
of the dark brown leaves all aquiver,
quiver, quiver.
I see the bright blue sky
beaming in front of me,
and I hear the buzzing of the bee.
The leaves grow,
the flowers bloom
and then I hear wedding bells
for a bride and groom.

Emily Clark (9)
East Bergholt CE (VC) Primary School

Moon

The light shone through the window
into the misty, murky dark.
In the silence grew the midnight,
lost was the song of the lark.
But in the growing midnight
something dark had stirred.
A wolf upon the hillside
rising like an early bird.
The howl flew through the treetops
into the golden field,
and there that night a little shrew ran
under the barley and squealed.
Suddenly from over the mountains
the dawn had begun,
through the window instead
shone the glittering sun.

Genevieve Kotarska (10)
East Bergholt CE (VC) Primary School

From An Aeroplane Window

(Inspired by 'From a Railway Carriage' by Robert Louis Stevenson)

Faster than a train, faster than a car,
Taking off at three hundred miles per hour.
Everything flashes past so fast,
Every second gone is now the past.

Up, up, up and away,
Going on holiday in the middle of May,
Looking out of the window I can see,
Bright lights flashing as if they are winking at me.

The clouds fly past in different shapes,
This plane is posh, we've all got drapes.
Down below, on solid land,
I can see a football stand.

Over the sea, over the waves,
Under the water are some deep, dark caves.
Down below land in sight,
This must be the end of our flight.

Faster than a train, faster than a car,
Landing at three hundred miles per hour.
Everything flashes past so fast,
Now England is the past.

Samantha Ayrton & Grace Sanderson (9)
Fordham All Saints CE Primary School

From A Flying Land Buggy

(Inspired by 'From a Railway Carriage' by Robert Louis Stevenson)

Children riding on electric scooters,
While others play on their computers.
Skyscrapers reaching up, shadowing the land,
There's a concert over there, with a rock star band.
The green is disappearing!

Travelling at 240mph
Hey! I've just caught a glimpse of the Eiffel Tower!
Fancy restaurants, fancy cars,
A planet museum in the shape of Mars!
The green is disappearing!

The Euro train, with first class seats,
Loud music playing what a fantastic beat.
People using bank machines,
Shopaholics are very keen.
The green is disappearing!

I've just been out, for a little trip,
To the shops now I will nip.
I need some tea, I want some cake,
I've just seen a digger, digging up a lake.
The green has disappeared!

Kirsty French & Megan Griffiths (9)
Fordham All Saints CE Primary School

The Sunflower

The sunflowers dance in the wind,
The normally still leaves now rocking about like a ship in a storm,
Each knocking into another in turn like a row of dominoes.
Each over seven feet tall, shrinking to the view of a worm.

Quivering, as the wind strikes them down.
Suddenly, the rage of the storm passes
And a gentle breeze tips them side to side.

A bright yellow face looking around,
As though searching for a friend.
Amazing great green leaves
Swivel in every direction calmly . . . calmly.
The only word for this wonderful beauty.

Sam Griffiths (11)
Fordham All Saints CE Primary School

From A Concorde Window

(Inspired by 'From a Railway Carriage' by Robert Louis Stevenson)

Faster than me, faster than you,
Faster than anything that people can do,
Like a spear being thrown through the air,
Targeting to hit a hunted bear.

People swimming and sailing in the sea,
Look someone's caught a fish like a bee,
We're flying over the Great Wall of China,
And it's amazing, it's a great white tiger.

We're flying over Australia now,
There's a great big rugby crowd,
They've come to see the final of the rugby World Cup,
Jonny Wilkinson kicked the ball and it's going up.

We're almost at the airport now over in New Zealand,
We've travelled all the way from England,
It's an eight and a half hour trip,
Now we're miles away from Gatwick!

Alex Clancy (11) & Oliver Noon (10)
Fordham All Saints CE Primary School

Memories

There is a secret, cold and still,
Of memories, of lies, of spirits too.
Ghost faces battle in despair
Behind silver water one thousand memories swim,
As each puzzle turns each day cold,
The battles come back . . .

The day is unearthly blue and gold,
Birds fly high, cold and lost,
Each person is a trance like a silver wick,
The silvery water shimmers, a wind is coming,
Bodies hide like featherless chickens.

Everyone is calm, not afraid or happy,
Just normal and content in the green passage leading.

Hatty Nestor (10)
Fordham All Saints CE Primary School

The Sand And The Sea

The furious sea crashes down,
Leaving tracks and foam on the sand,
Like unplugging a bath and leaving all the bubbles in.
The miniature shells get crushed by the hooves
Of the sea's galloping horses,
Like dry leaves, split into pieces.
Waves upset the floor of the ocean,
Like a sandstorm under the water.
The creatures of the ocean graze past the seaweed,
Like the wind blowing at the trees.
Oil leaks out of the tank, polluting the clean sea,
Like pouring ink into pure water.
Under the sea the fish fight a losing battle,
Like armies without weapons.

Fiona Clifft (10)
Fordham All Saints CE Primary School

Maybe There's A Problem With Me!

I like to sing
but the world doesn't.
Maybe there's a problem with me!

I want to dance
but I can't.
Maybe there's a problem with me!

I like the trumpet,
I want to play.

I tried it out
but I got scared.
Maybe I can't do anything!

I like the piano,
I want to play,
oh that's fun.
There may not be a problem with me!

Emma Beard (11)
Great Bentley Primary School

It's Not Fair

We are at school and nobody's not
I want to throw snowballs a lot.

I want to build a snowman, then knock it down,
Then I want to escape to Colchester Town.

We're not allowed outside and it's so not fair,
At break you're not allowed to eat your pear.

We have to get a minibus,
But nobody does.

When we go home the snow will be gone,
We had to do work all day long.

In one way I wished it didn't snow
But in another I do.
It's so, so, so unfair, I just want to rip out my hair.

Peter Brough (10)
Great Bentley Primary School

The Princess' Wedding

The king once said,
'Bring me the head
Of the evil goblin man.'
Then throughout the population,
There had been a celebration,
With processions far and wide,
For the jolly groom and bride.
After happiness and joy
There'd been a baby boy.
But before all of this,
Before the baby, bride or kiss,
The evil goblin worked away,
Until the very end of day,
Then with much anticipation
He made a fine creation,
To gain the princess' heart,
So they would never be apart.

Sophie Armsby (10)
Great Bentley Primary School

Weather

The weather is yellow when she is joyful.
The weather is grey and blotchy when she is sad.
The weather is hopping when she is hailstoning.
The weather is as soft as down on a swan's back when she is merry.
The weather is dribbling when she is gloomy.

Loren Rowland (10)
Great Bentley Primary School

War

War was born in Iraq,
And he wears a jacket of bullets
And has poppies on his shoes,
His cousin, World War I is 4 years old,
And is German,
His dad, World War II is 6 years old
And is also German.
War is only a year old,
And War is consuming the tanks
And other machines,
War is exterminating the enemy,
His finger ready to pull the trigger.

With blood dripping from his hands,
With gunpowder in his lungs,
War has sung,
That the war has begun,
In Iraq.
War leaps to another place in the same country,
War doesn't care who he kills,
All he cares about
Is that he lives.

David Lazar (11)
Great Bentley Primary School

Winter

It is a windy day,
You're making me shiver,
Jack Frost has been here,
He is making me slither.
I can't feel my fingers,
I can't feel my toes,
Now you have given me a red nose.

Chantelle Fenton-Jones (11)
Great Bentley Primary School

Egyptians

E legant buildings
G ranules of sand blind people's eyes
Y ou feel the small scorching flies
P eople work till the bell rings
T ired as they are the bird sings
I n the fiery sun
A pharaoh watches till the work is done
N asty people slave away
S un sets, with a ray.

Matthew Clarke (10)
Great Bentley Primary School

There's Snow In The Playground

There's snow in the playground,
All fluffy and white,
A boy threw a snowball at me
With all his might!

There's snow in the playground,
It's all slushy now,
The boy who threw the snowball
Has been having a big row.

There's snow in the playground,
My toes are nearly off with cold
The snow's been out for ages now,
I'm sure it's full of mould!

There's snow in the playground
And I've lost my scarf
I'm absolutely freezing
Playing on the snow raft.

There's snow in the playground,
My teeth are really chattering,
But it's great throwing snowballs
So that's now what's mattering.

Mikaela Barber (11)
Great Bentley Primary School

Harry Potter

Walking along the Hogwart's corridors,
Is mean and nasty Snape,
He's the teacher of potions,
In his long black cape.

Here comes the teacher of Transfiguration,
Professor McGonagall,
Striding along with noise making echoes,
In her dark green shawl.

Here is a know-it-all,
Hermione clever-clogs,
Slyly chewing on something,
Maybe chocolate frogs.

There goes Ron Weasley,
Harry's best ever friend,
They'll always stay together,
Until the very end.

And last of all there's Harry,
Flying on the Quidditch pitch,
He zooms and skims across the sky
And catches the Golden Snitch.

Lily Fritz (10)
Great Bentley Primary School

Winter

Winter wears only white,
It drifts around hunting during the night,
Icy cold winds creeping under the door,
Freezing drafts sliding over the floor.

Zoë Monger (10)
Great Bentley Primary School

Ipswich Town

When I go to see Ipswich play
I feel nervous.
Will we win or lose?
I hope we win!
The turnstile goes round
Like a wheel on my bike.
When my ticket gets ripped
It makes me feel sad.
I go to get my seat,
I feel happy . . . but sad.
I think I am nervous!
But when it is half-time
I feel rapturous!
Me and Dad get a steak pie.
Dad gets a pint.
I look forward to the second half.

Lee Kerridge (10)
Great Bentley Primary School

The Weird Man

Once there was a man
Who was wearing a vest
He thought he was the best
He needed a rest
He was so stressed
He didn't like to get dressed
He didn't like a guest
His brother was a pest
His bird had a nest.

Mark Mullenger (11)
Great Bentley Primary School

Buffy Kennings

Big fighter,
Vamp hater,
Key hider,
Spike lover,
High kicker,
Good looker,
Big thumper,
Small dater,
Big faker,
Law breaker,
Night lover,
Big staker,
Non drinker,
Make-up user,
Faith hater,
Big monsters
(Easy to fight).

Ellis Davies (11)
Great Bentley Primary School

Bicycle

A bike has two wheels,
When you go fast it feels
Absolutely brilliant.

My mate burned his Apollo,
His heart did not feel hollow,
Right afterwards.

Up a hill you need your gears,
Otherwise you'll lose your ears,
That'll hurt.

A bike has two brakes,
You'll go into lakes
Without them.

Andrew Blackman (11)
Great Bentley Primary School

Football Haikus

Football is so great
I play football every week
I play for Clacton.

Becks is my favourite
Beckham plays for Real Madrid
Beckham plays midfield.

Becks' son is Brooklyn
He is four years tomorrow
Becks has Romeo.

One of the Spice Girls
He married Victoria,
They love each other.

Ruud van Nistelrooy
He is a wicked striker
He's a golden boot.

Ruud van Nistelrooy
Ruud van Nistelrooy is best
He beats defenders.

He controls the ball
Then he gets a great shot in
It's in top corner.

Man U 1-0 up
Against rivals Arsenal
Can they score again?

Goalie saves the ball
Defenders are at the back
Midfield are centre.

They keep the structure
Or they may go up and down
Strikers have good shots.

Ryan Gooch (10)
Great Bentley Primary School

Chelsea FC

Chelsea are the very best,
Some games they might have messed,
Running up half the pitch,
Then scoring against Norwich.

Chelsea stand boiling heat,
Especially with sweaty feet,
Man U hit from half the field,
Chelsea still had to shield.

Hasselbaink's power shots,
Scores lots and lots,
Zola's perfect flick
Got Chelsea the tick.

When it comes near the end,
Chelsea score with a bend,
When it comes to full time,
Chelsea start counting time.

Jonathan Hartley (11)
Great Bentley Primary School

Animals

Ten animals burping
Nine dogs barking
Eight cats miaowing
Seven donkeys saying eeyore
Six monkeys swinging
Five pigs rolling
Four kangaroos bouncing
Three cats purring
Two bats flying
One rabbit hopping.

Anna-Leigh Atwell (8)
John Ray Junior School

Medieval Times In Rhyme

The knights are ready to collide,
The king has to decide,
To attack or defend,
Either way he cannot offend.

Catapults are ready to attack,
Not like the war in Iraq.
Arrows are flying everywhere,
Knights with swords are fighting with such care.

We need to feed,
Their trusty steeds,
Knights, spear throwers, men with bow and arrows,
Swordsmen and knights with their trusty steeds,
No gardeners needed to pull weeds.

The enemy is leaving, we've won,
Wait, one still comes braver than everyone,
The castle walls are weakening, what shall we do?
I know what we shall do,
We'll get every man and knight in the castle
That's what we shall do.

We have won,
We are better than everyone,
You have lost,
Now you have to pay the cost.

Luke Prow (9)
John Ray Junior School

Cars

Some cars are fast,
Some cars are slow,
There are all different types of cars,
Like my dad's Mondeo.

Stefan Gray (8)
John Ray Junior School

The Seasons

In spring flowers start to bloom,
In spring blossom begins to grow on trees,
Animals awake from hibernation.

In summertime the sun is really hot,
It's time to get swimming costumes on
And go swimming at the beach.

In autumn leaves begin to fall off trees,
The cold starts to come in the windy days of autumn,
We can fly kites in the park.

In winter it's very cold and the last leaves fall off trees,
Sometimes the snow comes in winter,
Then it's spring again in a new year!

Christopher Stone (8)
John Ray Junior School

The Lion

He has claws like razors
He has a big fluffy mane like a bunch of pillows
He has teeth like sharp knives
And a roar like thunder.

Connor Vickery (8)
John Ray Junior School

My Cat

My cat is a female.
She has a long tail.
She likes tuna with mayonnaise.
She has soft paws.
She has razor-sharp claws.
She is as ginger as gingerbread.
She likes to play
And pounce on my bed.

Tommy Guilder (8)
John Ray Junior School

In Spring

In spring, birds are chirping,
Eggs are hatching,
Blossom on the trees,
Kids are playing,
When leaves blow in the breeze.

In spring, lambs play in the fields,
Flowers bloom,
People go swimming,
Shoots in the meadow,
While people are saying, 'Hello! hello!'

Charlotte Tuff (8)
John Ray Junior School

My Cat

She plays during the day,
She sleeps in front of the fire,
After drinking her milk,
Her skin is like silk,
She is as sweet as sugar,
And likes to chase mice.
She purrs on my lap,
Her yellow eyes glow in the dark.

Charlotte Bradley (9)
John Ray Junior School

Winter

The trees are bare
They have icicles for hair
The snow is deep
The animals are asleep
It's so cold
I feel like I live in the North Pole.

Georgia Peagram (8)
John Ray Junior School

Spring And Autumn

In springtime buds are on the trees,
Kids swimming and playing everywhere,
Baby lambs born in the stable,
Bluebirds singing while honeybees are wondering,
Eggs hatching in every farm,
All flowers blooming.

Kids all go to sleep now
For the next day will be autumn.

Leaves fall from every tree,
Days get shorter and shorter,
Kids go in to play in front of the fire,
Mums start cooking a nice hot dinner.

Melisso Bonito (9)
John Ray Junior School

An Elephant Comes To Tea

I saw an elephant walking one day,
He had big ears and he heard me say,
'I wonder if he'd like to come to tea?'
He said, 'Are you asking me?'

We went back home and made bread and jam,
He asked, 'Can I have cheese and ham?'

He ate it quick, so very fast,
I tried my best but ended last,
We ate so much we looked so big,
When I looked again he'd turned into a pig!

Jessica Harris (9)
John Ray Junior School

Spring

Spring is when leaves sway in the breeze,
Birds grow on trees,
While farmers grow their corn
New babies are being born.
Birds singing, buzzing bees,
Flowers spinning, bells ringing,
Eggs hatching, people scratching.

Laura McDonnell (9)
John Ray Junior School

My Dogs

I have two dogs called Scooby and Kai,
I really do love them but I don't know why.

They go in my room and chew all my toys,
They really are two naughty boys.

I throw their ball high up into the sky,
And I know I will love them to the day I die.

Penny Buchan (9)
John Ray Junior School

Friends

F un times when we play together
R uined times when we break up
I nvisible friends
E xciting games
N o more tears because I'll look after you
D o you trust me?
S pecial friends forever.

Shannen Hamilton (9)
John Ray Junior School

The War Of Iraq

It's midnight on a warm summer's night
I am sitting here with fright
And holding my legs tight.

Bullets and bombs go past me
Helicopter and Harrier jets are in the sky,
A missile is heading my way
Oh no! It missed.

Right in front of my eyes
People are being injured and killed
A young baby cries
As her mother lies on the ground and dies.

I have no food and my home is destroyed
I can't find my family
There are bombs and guns surrounding me
But I just want to be free.

My ears can take no more noise
And I have left all of my toys.

Suddenly there's a gun to my head
Have I been found?
Will I be fed?
Maybe I should have stayed in bed
Soldiers run and shout at each other
I just think I want my mother.

Will this be the end?
Will I ever be able to play in the park?
Or will I just die in the war of Iraq?

Samuel Stirrup (8)
John Ray Junior School

Bunny

I bought a little bunny,
She didn't cost a lot of money,
But she was very funny,
With her little white feet
And she loved a juicy carrot as a treat.

Amber Baker (8)
John Ray Junior School

Anna-Leigh

My best friend Anna-Leigh . . .
Has hair like the colour of the sun,
It is as long as a skirt.
She is as small as a garden gnome.
She is funny like a monkey.
Her smile is as wide as a bus.
She runs as quickly as a dog.
She is as beautiful as a butterfly.

Sarah Jeanes (8)
John Ray Junior School

Oh Beautiful Butterfly

Oh beautiful butterfly, with its beautiful colourful wings,
Your wings are as delicate as sherbet in the wind.

I know I'm not meant to touch you, but your body looks so soft,
I can't resist being kissed by a beautiful butterfly like you.

If you caught the flu I'd keep you in a cage so I can keep you safe,
You can have a sleep in the noon and I'll wake you very soon.

Kaya Tokkan (9)
John Ray Junior School

The Purple Baloo

The purple baloo,
The purple baloo.

An animal that's new
To nature and you.

The purple baloo,
The purple baloo.

Eats jam tarts
And sky-blue larks.

The purple baloo,
The purple baloo.

Lives in Fagaloo,
Goes, 'Waa waa woo!'

The purple baloo,
The purple baloo.

Climbs trees,
Hides in leaves.

The purple baloo,
The purple baloo.

Just for fun
They jump on everyone.

Peter Warner (9)
John Ray Junior School

Weather

The sun is shining high in the sky,
It comes out in the day, when it's dry,
A rainbow appears when it's wet and sunny,
I've been told it has a pot of gold
But I think it has a pot of money.

Khia Robinson (9)
John Ray Junior School

Winter

Winter is the time of year,
When it often snows,
And flakes fly everywhere,
When the cold wind blows.

Winter is the time of year,
When there is a lot of breeze,
Which is when you catch a cold,
That makes you cough and sneeze.

Winter is the time of year,
When it pours down with rain,
It floods down the roads,
And disappears down the drain.

Winter is the time of year,
When the snow turns into ice,
Stay indoors by the fire,
Where it's cosy and nice.

Winter is the time of year,
Bare are all the trees,
The freezing wind has swirled around
And taken all the leaves.

Lucy Rae Mallott (9)
John Ray Junior School

Chinese New Year

Kerry is a monkey,
Mum is a sheep.

Dad is a dog
And Harry is a rat.

These are the animals of the Chinese New Year,
I'll say it again so that you can hear!

Kerry Muscutt (9)
John Ray Junior School

My Best Friend Amber

My best friend Amber is as pretty as a butterfly,
Is as cute as a button,
She's as funny as a clown,
She's as small as a garden gnome,
Her eyes are as blue as the sky,
She dresses like a princess
And is as clever as a bookworm.

Lauren Seymour (9)
John Ray Junior School

Some Dogs

Some dogs are nice,
Some dogs are kind,
They can almost read your mind.
They know if you are sad or blue
They come and snuggle up to you.

Sophie Ryder (8)
John Ray Junior School

Sunny Hills

I once looked upon sunny hills,
Wearing my dress with lovely frills.
Watching the day go by my window sill,
Thinking of my boyfriend Bill.
As I have some time to kill
I shall go to the watermill.

Nicole Reid (9)
John Ray Junior School

Silly

Who keeps on being silly
Maybe it's my teddy, Billy.
He fell out of bed
And hurt his head
Oh what a silly Billy.

James Hedger (8)
John Ray Junior School

My Brother

My brother smells,
He goes to my mum and tells.

He kicks, he spits,
He calls me very thick.
Apart from that he's alright.

He plays with Spiderman
And reads Desperate Dan.

When he's my chum
It can be very fun.

Zoë Edwards (9)
John Ray Junior School

Feeling Ill

I just woke up in my bed,
I think I've lost my head.
I'll end up feeling like I'm dead,
I hope in Heaven they have bread!

Ife Fayanju (9)
John Ray Junior School

Leanne

L is for loving, love to share.
E is for enthusiasm, do things with flair.
A is for attractive, clever and smart.
N is for neat, a caring sweetheart.
N is for noisy, always on the go.
E is for enjoyable, watching you grow.

Leanne Wilson (8)
John Ray Junior School

Limerick

There once was a horse from Mersea,
Who likes going down to Bertie's.
The horse liked eating hay
He ate hay every day.
That was the story from Mersea.

Thomas Wargent (8)
Mersea Island School

Limerick

There once was a girl called Jessie
Who had a pet dog called Bessie
She took her for a walk
She barks instead of talks and
Wags her tail as she walks.
Now Jessie is just like Bessie.

Jessica Royce (9)
Mersea Island School

Limerick

There once was a furry fat rat
Who was scared of a bat
He caught a bad chill
And became very ill
At the sight of the bat he went splat!

Luke Haxell (9)
Mersea Island School

Limerick

There once was a cat from England
And he loved to play in the sand
He lay on the beach
Got washed out of reach
So I gave him a helping hand.

Toni-Jane Parker (9)
Mersea Island School

Limerick

There once was this girl called Betty
She ate her dog called Spaghetti
But her dog was very bad
So she spat it out, quite mad
And Spaghetti flew like confetti.

Taylor Madden (9)
Mersea Island School

My Friend Jess

There was a young girl called Jess
She could be an absolute mess
She loves to wear trousers
For hours and hours
But would never wear a short dress.

Jack Sheeran (8)
Mersea Island School

The Grumpy Groany Pony

There once was a grumpy pony
And he was forever moany
No one could ever sit
Not even for a bit
That was the life of a groany pony.

Danielle Fautley (8)
Mersea Island School

Limerick

There once was a dolphin called Ellie
She was playful and called Ellie Nellie
But she was very naughty
She was very naughty
She's very playful is Ellie Nellie.

Lucinda Cawdron (8)
Mersea Island School

Snake And The Rake

There once was a slithery yellow snake
Who was hit by a very sharp rake
He was as tall as a door
Now he's only one foot four
But he still likes a bit of cake.

Mark Halsey (9)
Mersea Island School

Limerick

There once was a dog from France
He wished he could learn how to dance
He tried at a disco
In San Francisco
And ended up in a trance.

Harry Ager (9)
Mersea Island School

A Dog From New York

There once was a dog from New York
He hated the taste of pork
He couldn't stand the ham
He whacked his head on the pram
And he hated the sound of a cork.

Hannah Wilkin (8)
Mersea Island School

Limerick

There once was a man from Brazil
Who became incredibly ill
He rolled in hot yellow sand
And he cut his sweaty hand
Then he became very, very ill.

Ellie Dawson (9)
Mersea Island School

Limerick

There was a young girl called Maisy
Who rhymes with Daisy and Maisy
She loves to play in sand
Even likes her smelly land
And she likes days that are hazy.

Amy Wilkin (8)
Mersea Island School

Limerick

There once was a fox from Brazil
And he was going to be ill
He thought he wasn't at all
But he ran into a wall
No wonder he felt so ill.

Ben Lake (8)
Mersea Island School

My Oak Tree

Hear the oak drop
Its brown, crisp leaves.
An acorn drops from the tree,
The touch of the
Hard wooden stems.
It asks for warmth,
Children climbing.
Picking acorns.
Animals rushing
Up and down
Squirrels rushing,
Finding food.
Foxes hiding
In the roots.
Woodlice climbing
In and out.

Charlotte Taylor (9)
Mersea Island School

The Pine Tree

The spiky leaves whistling,
The pine tree is crying for water.
Its branches are twisting.
The cones falling to the ground.

Leaves are a canopy,
Roots lie down in the soil.
Trunk becoming bigger,
Needles prick everything.

Katie Whiting (8)
Mersea Island School

Seeing Earth From Space

Seeing the Earth, 24 hours a day
Is a pleasure, I can say.
Stars and space shuttles, zooming past
And hopefully, it won't be the last!
It's fun to do a Peter Pan across the room
And the zero gravity makes us zoom.

Seeing the Earth, 24 hours a day
Is something I can say.
Seeing the stars and the sun, going around your head.
Makes you want to go to bed.
As we began to enter the moon's atmosphere,
I began to have quite a fear.

Seeing the Earth, 24 hours a day,
Is fantastic I can say.
Comets and asteroids going by
And they were very high.
Seeing the Earth, 24 hours a day is
Excellent, I can say!

Josh Gosling (10)
Mersea Island School

Stars And The Moon

The stars and the moon gather together,
To make a good show.
No longer we wait
No longer we hate.
Because the world is a better place,
Tears have gone,
Happiness is out.

Laura Henderson (9)
Mersea Island School

Me As A Pyramid

There I am
Standing all alone
Pointing up into space.
I can hear the slaves singing,
Wishing to be free.
Why am I the one who has to be lonely?
I look down and see
There are no men anymore.

I look around
And all I can see is sand, sand, sand!
There is a crumpled, damaged statue.
It has fallen into the deep smooth sand.
The world is dark, windy and silent
The everlasting sun has gone . . .

Alice Saleh (8)
Mersea Island School

Space

'All units go! 3, 2, 1 lift-off!'
Off the rocket goes,
All mankind's labour.
Teamship getting the rocket ready,
Trust and hope that the space shuttle goes
Love with the astronaut supporting them
All the way.
The astronaut's dream came true.
They work but they just can't stop thinking.
What's it like in space?

Liam Moriarty (9)
Mersea Island School

Oak Tree

Leaves rustle and whisper in the wind,
Acorns fall in thousands.
Enormous trunk covered with ivy.
A tree good for climbing,
So tall it touches the sky,
Roots spreading underfoot,
Red leaves as well as yellow and brown.
Oak groaning for water.

Juliette Spence (9)
Mersea Island School

Untitled

One minute to lift-off . . . Houston, we have lift-off!
I can feel the G-force throwing me back in my seat.
Gradually I feel weightless.
Ten minutes later, I want to come back.
As we enter the new atmosphere
The rocket burns with fury.

Reece Bonds (9)
Mersea Island School

A Wood

Lots of trees rustling in the wind,
Making shadows on the path.
Hazelnuts dropping to the ground,
Sycamore seeds whirl away with the help of the wind,
Pine cones lying on the floor leaving a lovely smell in the air,
A beautiful red rose lying on the ground.
Trees making shade and a home for birds to live.
Animals grateful for the space it gives.

Blyth Huxley (8)
Mersea Island School

The Oak Tree

Acorns falling to the ground,
Bending branches in the wind.
The oak, wanting water,
Roots lying in the soil
Drinking water when it rains.
The branches, mostly broken.
The giant leaves always red.
Seeds falling off the tree
And a little shoot grows.

Rebecca Southward (9)
Mersea Island School

Storm

Leaves were beckoning me in,
Branches calling me in deep.
The wind howled behind me,
Suddenly thunder roared,
Lightning cracked through the inky sky.
Trunks were charred, leaves of orange,
The wood was crackling with fire.

Hetty Baalham (9)
Mersea Island School

The Sun - Kennings

Light giver
Space liver
Planet holder
Country folder
Trouble maker
Day breaker
Planet maker.

Liam Bond (9)
Mersea Island School

Zooming Through Space

Zooming through space
Nothing but black.
Ten minutes later, they want
To come back.
Oh wait!
The moon, so cold and dusty.
Nothing but sand hills,
On the way up, nothing but silence
On the way down.
Coming through the atmosphere
Like a train, at full speed.
Splash into the sea.

Josh Moncur (9)
Mersea Island School

Space

It's wonderful having friends,
They're lovely.
You can enjoy journeys
Soaring through the sky.

See Mars and Jupiter
Astronauts that fly.
You can dance and sing in the catch of your eye.
You dream about stars which are passing by.
When you're tired of floating around -
You can fly like a bird to golden sand.
Walk through a field with pink and yellow flowers,
Till you arrive with your powers.

Chloe Mussett (10)
Mersea Island School

Stranded

Many people go on trips
Through the widening road
Before you know it, you are lost
So they have to pay the cost.

We are in a safari desert
No wind, no food, no nothing
Just sand.

We don't know how long we will last;
Ten days, two weeks?
I don't know!
Why did we come on this trip?

We are dying quicker, minute by minute
All I ask is for a drink.
We are going to die, I cannot bare to think.

When I try to sleep
All I hear is howling
And the freezing wind upon my face.
Will I die or will I live to see another day?

Jack Goldring (10)
Mersea Island School

The Ancient Greeks

A journey of discovery
To the Ancient Greeks.
Athena and the gods
Standing on their peaks.
Zeus, like a flame
Burning on a candle.
Athena like a waterfall
Bravely flowing in her sandals.

Yasmin Gillingham (9)
Mersea Island School

Space So Black

Rockets fly high
In the black, bright sky
The moon so bright
It will blind your eye
Fire, so hot
It will boil your blood.
Space so black
With little white dots.
Stars bright,
It's like a light in the night.
Energy so fast,
Like a cheetah, running.
The sun so hot,
It's like a giant fireball.

Sayman Ismail (10)
Mersea Island School

The Earth Is Like A Big Sweet

Solar system, like big chocolate buttons,
Speed, like a rally car in a race.
Heat, like a fire glowing on my face.
Force, like someone springing from a bed.
Space, like a black hole.
Rockets, like children screaming,
Playing in the playground.

The Earth is like a big sweet,
But it would take forever to eat!

Lorna Cairns (9)
Mersea Island School

One Small Step For Man

One small step for man
One small step towards our destiny,
One small step onto the forbidden planet,
Where no man has been before.

One small leap for history,
One small leap for freedom.
One small leap and it's all over,
The task is nearly completed.

One giant leap to success,
One giant leap to eliminate this voyage.
One giant leap for life,
This day will never be forgotten
From this moment onwards.

'One small step for man
A giant leap for mankind'.

Everything starts with one small step.

Charlotte Boyle (11)
Mersea Island School

I've Been To Space And Back

I've been to space and back
The universe was black.
I've been to Mars and bought a car,
To get back to the human race.

The museums were great,
We were late.
But it didn't matter at all -
Because, there was Athena
Standing alone, powerful and tall.

Ben Pullen-Appleby (10)
Mersea Island School

Nocturnal People

Rockets flying in
Air like a cork
From a bottle

Nocturnal people
Muster with the
Rockets like bees
Muster with flowers

Rockets in the air
Encircled by planets
Like an orange
Encircled by skin

Space people
Wear nappies
Like babies

Down from
Space they will
Probably prosper.
Like passing your GCSEs.
What they did was good,
But they wondered -
What was for tea?

Daisy Sherwood (10)
Mersea Island School

Untitled

D ragon flying in the sky
R ing of claws
A nd of fire
G loomy sky
O verheating sun
N o people in the village.

Dominic Cirne (9)
Mersea Island School

A Journey Through Space

Rocky temples like a stone on the ground
Ancient temples which will be found
A journey through space
Like a black sheet of paper.
A journey through space
Like planets meeting each other
A journey of discovery
Like Earth, moon and sun.
A journey of discovery
Like the sun, shining on.

Kerry Ward (10)
Mersea Island School

A School Trip

Space is like swimming
Greece is hot,
We went on a school trip
And learned a lot.
Shooting stars
Are like balls of fire.
Greek temples get
Higher and higher.
How I felt was
Really very special.
On the coach
It was like a kettle.

Charlotte Guest (9)
Mersea Island School

The Sky

The moon is like a bouncy ball
With a big cheesy grin.
A shuttle is like a banana
Peeling its skin.
An astronaut is like a big moth,
Learning to fly.
The stars are like diamonds,
Sparkling in the sky.
The planets are like bowling balls
With lots of different colours
I say goodbye to all the sky and
Hope to see you again, some night.

Alex Birch (10)
Mersea Island School

Now We Know

The Greeks lived
Very long ago
We dug up pots
And now we know
They built temples
For their gods
They told stories
Like Theseus
They made mosaics
Like beautiful jigsaws
We dug up pots
And now we know.

Joseph Peter Vince (10)
Mersea Island School

Space, Greece, London, My Journey Of Discovery

Space looks like a sheet of black paper,
Stars look silver and sit in the sky.
Multicoloured planets sit still as ice,
But who is the maker, may I ask?
Rockets then come and disturb the universe
But when they leave, peace returns.

The Greek temples stand tall and proud,
Like a boastful queen of the sky.
'I wish I could see a real Greek temple,'
Say you and I.
Under the hot burning sun is where
The temples lie.
We are tiny ants, while the temples stand
So tall and high.

My journey of discovery
Through a lovely huge place.
My journey of discovery
Looks at Big Ben's clock face!
My journey of discovery
Through a mystical city.
My journey of discovery
Where Greek pillars were pretty.
My day of magic was over,
I was sad.
But to get home to my bed
I was extremely glad!

Abbie Heathcote (10)
Mersea Island School

A Journey Of Discovery

Fast rockets, like athletes in a race
Fire, like the blazing sun in space

Big Ben like a rocket about to take off
The Millennium Dome, very well shown
Many discoverers, digging up the ground
Lots of Greek towns, making up a mound

So come along and join me
In a journey of discovery.

Luke Dawson (10)
Mersea Island School

Moon Walk

Space, a magical place
Going in and around galaxies and stars
A new adventure every day
Brave astronauts, risking their lives
Putting up satellites
Setting up laboratories
Space stations for research.

Neil Armstrong's first moonwalk
The atmosphere was electric
Full of sound and excitement.

Matthew Wilkin (10)
Mersea Island School

Space

A rocket like a dolphin shooting in the sky,
Launch pad engines like a dragon's roar.
Soars through Earth's atmosphere,
Space, like a black wolf leaping so high.

Shayne Lacey (10)
Mersea Island School

Space

When you look up in the sky
You see all the planets passing by
There's Jupiter, Mars and many more
I start to rise until I soar.

I feel like a real astronaut
Floating in the sky
I don't feel heavy, way up high.

It feels like it's all a dream
And none of its true
I can't even remember if the sky is blue.

I've been up here so long now
I'm getting a little dizzy
Maybe I should come back down
To human gravity.

Holly Wells (10)
Mersea Island School

Laughter And fun

A journey of discovery
Laughter and fun
A journey of discovery
Joy for all who come
Big Ben is staring down on us
As we pass by on the bus
Another half an hour passes
Then we arrive -
With the other classes.

Kirsty Ward (10)
Mersea Island School

My Dreams

My dream is to be a veterinary surgeon
Living in Birch Village.

My dream is to have my very own farm
With animals of all kinds.

My dream is for the world to live in peace
And harmony.

My dream is for world hunger, drought and floods,
All to be banished.

My dream is for all chemical bombs to be destroyed
And more money for hospitals.

My dreams are a light which never goes out,
Burning on and on, forever.

Emily Birch (11)
Mersea Island School

If I Was A Pyramid

Many years of staring into space,
Hearing the lonely groaning of slaves.
Panting men, women and children.
Hearing the rocket sounding like somebody saying, shhh!
I point up to the protected gods.
I am a golden tomb for the shielded people,
Many people lie inside, cold, grey and dull,
Suddenly, I start collapsing,
Melting into the gingery-yellow, sand.

Abigail Birkett (9)
Mersea Island School

Trees

Pears fall to the ground
Wild apples hang around
Limes glide in the wind
Ash starts to grow again
Palms wave in the breezes
Sloes burst open their skin
Oaks are dormant in the cold
Acorns lie in their cups
Sweet chestnuts grow their spikes.

Georgina Diprose (8)
Mersea Island School

Oak Tree

Oak standing rigid through a storm,
Winds, drought and dying for water.
Life brittle.
Acorns falling like a bomb,
A crush in the wind.
The noise squeaking
Leaves on a branch
So all the people can point and stare.
My seeds make lovely fruit to eat,
My sweet apple
Tastes sweet to eat.

Sam Dow (9)
Mersea Island School

Oak Tree

One little acorn in its cup
In a tree way, way up.
Every day it grows,
In dark, leafy places.
Every day begins
The same old races.
One acorn in its cup,
Departing here and further up.
The tree is strong,
Feels like fire.
The tree protects the land
Some people give a hand.

Sophie Innocent (9)
Mersea Island School

The Willow's Thirst

The whimpering willow whines for water,
Dangles down to the dried-up riverbed.
It hangs lower than it ever has before.
Save it from destruction,
The people think it's dead.
It sleeps, waiting for the rain to come.
The willow is frightened for it knows its fate,
Men come!

It's raining,
An amazing sight is born.
They leave the tree to its own eternity,
The tree is fine. It waits for another life.

Rebekah Boreham (8)
Mersea Island School

A Hidden Place

Somewhere up above the clouds,
Is a place that no one came to see.
Rockets fly there, so what can it be?
Astronauts float around and bump up and down,
While their food floats around.
When they take up from the air,
Their hands float everywhere.
So now you know
That it could be
Space!

May Leverington (10)
Mersea Island School

Soaring Through Space

Soaring through space
Past comets and ships.
Looking back at the Earth
Seeing green, yellow and blue.
Discovering the white moon
Panicked by the red giant.
Moving into a black hole.
An asteroid knocks us out.
Trained to keep control.

Reece Waring (10)
Mersea Island School

Flying Through Space

High in space the astronaut looked down,
Soaring, towering, elegantly spying on Earth.
Thinking about the galaxy.
Black looming around me.
Behold Mars dawdling past my porthole,
They think they've seen it all down on Earth.
But it has only just begun.

Jack Bentley (9)
Mersea Island School

Blast-Off!

Blast-off! We are now in space!
Space, a giant black hole.
Planets, different coloured balls,
Rocket, a sword with height.
Flames, raging orange light.
Right now, landing.
We say goodbye,
To mysterious planets
Way up high.

Emma Kemp (10)
Mersea Island School

The Mighty Vulcan

A journey of discovery, amazement and fun,
A journey of planets, Earth, moon and sun.

A journey of discovery, yet to know,
Stands the mighty Vulcan, further than Pluto.

Matthew O'Brien (10)
Mersea Island School

When I Went To Space And Back

When I went to space and back
The universe was like a cave,
Extremely black,
With my spacesuit and my nappy,
I felt really happy.
When I went to space and back.

Megan Eley (9)
Mersea Island School

Planets Do Not Chose To Move

Oh Mercury, oh Venus
You are near to Earth.
You didn't choose to be far away,
But you chose to be by Earth's bay.
If you chose to be far away
Earth would be on its way.
But planets do not move,
So let's just stay.
Okay?

Ben Davies (9)
Mersea Island School

A Black World

Space like a black world
Planets like different coloured footballs
Rockets like shiny metal
With heat and flames
Stars like bits of glitter
Space!

Joshua Gunning (9)
Mersea Island School

Searching For Mars

Space is a massive place,
Where you can soar like a comet.
Glide like a plane,
Inside the spacecraft, worried, scared
Then *pow!* Off like a roller coaster,
Going round the galaxy.
Looking around,
Excitement all round.
Watching out of the window,
Thousands of stars floating around.
Now it's time to go outside
And to see what is on Mars!

Ben Cirne (11)
Mersea Island School

Earth In Space

Ten seconds to blast-off
We're going into space.
A shiny piece of silver
Triple rockets like colourful fireworks.
Two minutes later, pitch-black, then millions of stars.
The moon is like a big piece of cheese,
Astronauts float in a moonwalk
No gravity,
Moon landing, people cheered.

Nicholas Capon (11)
Mersea Island School

Space

Blast-off! A flash of light,
Bright stars and planets
The rocket stops in mid-space.
You feel as light as a feather,
It's hard to feel the ground.
It's hard to eat and hard to sleep
So what I say is, lie back and enjoy.

George Green (11)
Mersea Island School

Dark Space

In the dark passages of space,
Entering the quiet lands of the galaxy,
Gravity loses control.
Magic glows all around,
The Earth is an amazing place!

Gary Wright (10)
Mersea Island School

Friends

Friends are the guys who make my life complete,
Friends are our family that we choose for ourselves,
Friends never leave you when you're feeling down,
Friends never push you to the ground.
Friends always hear you when you cry out,
Friends never tease or mess about,
Friends are the people I can't live without.

Lewis O'Sullivan
Mersea Island School

I Would Like . . .

I would like to be a great football player,
I would like to be better at golf,
I would like to be an animal expert,
Kind of like that guy Rolf.

I would like to be a happy chappy,
I would like some more trustworthy friends,
I would like for them all to be happy,
This is where the story ends.

Scott Shean (10)
Mersea Island School

Journeys

Many people take a trip
Along a winding road.
They find that they are lost,
So they have to pay the cost.

Some go to Africa on a safari,
Getting led in a tour,
When suddenly they get a surprise
When a snake looks them in the eyes.

Many go to London
To see Big Ben.
Some stay at home
And miss the Millennium Dome.

Luke Innocent (10)
Mersea Island School

Journey Into Space

3, 2, 1, blast-off,
We're on our way to the moon,
We'll be there very soon.
The whole shuttle was one big vibration,
While looking down seeing the nation.
This is great fun, while in a line one by one.
Ready for touch down, won't be long.
No sound.
One bang, we hit the ground.
Holding tight, trying to stay still,
Floating around while following drill.
Feeling nervous, looking at the open door,
Staring out all I can say is, 'Cor.'
Great big holes I could fall down,
But I still want to look around.
The change in gravity makes me lose weight,
It is very hard to walk straight.
A good look around, so much to see,
Back in the spaceship we now have to be.
The journey back we now make,
A giant step for mankind we take.

Charlie Pryke (10)
Mersea Island School

Space

Space is a place that we are always trying to conquer.
We have the best minds in the world,
Helping to break this force field of space,
That mysterious place.
We have rockets and fuel to soar up
To that unknown world!

Natassja Fairbanks (10)
Mersea Island School

Aliens And Planets

What colour are the planets?
Are they black and blue,
Yellow, green or purple? I don't know, do you?
Do they have life or are they just plain,
Or are they covered in silver, sapphire and gold?
Do they have air, or is it cold?
Can you float, like in space?

What colour are the aliens?
Are they yellow and blue with pink spots,
Not like me and you?
Can they fly or walk,
Or do they just breathe?
Do they eat things like me and you?

Max Rampling (11)
Mersea Island School

Friendship

Friendship is a treasure waiting to be found,
Longing for this fortune often lost in hatred,
People are broken, knowing that their hearts are empty,
Mankind could help if only it stopped to spare a thought.

When there are people feeling hurt or sad,
Stop and show them how to cope.
If you're at school, work or home,
Think before you speak, it may save a lot of grief.

If we all strive for friendship,
It would make life much easier to live.

Sarah Taylor (11)
Mersea Island School

Exploration Of Space

Stepping into the shuttle, feel the engines roar,
Leaving the Earth, higher, higher we soar.
Looking at Earth is a lovely sight,
A comet passing by gave me such a fright.
Passing black holes and exploding stars,
What's our destination? They say it is Mars.
With a bump we come to land,
I look out the porthole and see red, dry sand.
We step out of the shuttle and gaze all around,
Breathtaking, beautiful, it makes my heart pound.
A new way of life, so strange and so new,
I remember with sadness the Earth's morning dew.

Peter Lancefield (11)
Mersea Island School

We Wish There Was Peace . . .

We wish there was peace,
We wish there was friendship and loyalty.
Why can't we be friends?

We wish we could help,
We wish we could comfort.
Why can't we help?

We wish for the people
Who cannot wish for themselves.

Caitlin Devonish (10)
Mersea Island School

Space Knows And We Know

Space is like an unconquered country
Waiting for mankind to explore her.
She will know when the time is right
To let people enter into the realms of her world,
To let them capture her,
Make her their second nature,
With their advanced technology.
Space will be no more,
She will be ancient history.
She will be the place where
Everyone takes their holidays.
The space *we* know will be gone,
Just like us.

Lottie Turnbull-Swift (11)
Mersea Island School

Friendship

Friendship is a precious thing,
It's not something to hide.
You should share it with others,
Love and cherish it for life.

To have the strongest friendship,
You must be modest and kind.
You need generous quantities of love and care,
For your friendship to survive.

So if you're offered friendship,
It's a marvellous thing to have.
Don't dismiss it, it's a treasure
That money cannot buy.

Sophie Moul (11)
Mersea Island School

I Wish

I wish I didn't always fall,
I wish I was in fascinating France.
I wish I was perfectly tall,
I wish I could dance.
I wish I was happy,
I wish my brother wasn't shy,
I wish my sister didn't wear a nappy,
I wish my uncle didn't die.

Craig Bunyan (9)
Mersea Island School

Space

Travelling through the depth of the black wasteland
People wonder how and why we travelled into space.
Comets come into course, we wonder how they were made.
Black holes come, they are the deadliest things.
We look into them, but we can only see oblivion.
People want to become astronauts,
But what it takes is far too long.

Glen Sales (10)
Mersea Island School

Space

A n unexplored country
S eemingly endless,
T his country has no borders.
R ockets explore its infinite plains.
O n Earth, Ground Control keeps in touch.
N ebulas and stars are discovered by telescopes.
A stronauts at work.
U npopulated this country is.
T his country is space.

Thomas Ashmore (11)
Mersea Island School

Alone On The Horizon

Alone on the horizon,
With nothing to eat or drink.
They lay around weeping,
Hoping tomorrow will soon come!

They travel and travel
Until they can't walk
To keep their spirits up,
They can do nothing but talk.

Missing their families,
Desperate for a home.
Why is life like this?
They're out there alone!

Laura Chalklin (11)
Mersea Island School

World Peace

If there were peace all around,
There would be no wars.
If there were no wars,
People wouldn't die.
If there was harmony,
Trees would be safe.
If there were no trees,
The world would be empty like the night sky.
If there was peace all around,
We would be safe.

Sam Ward (10)
Mersea Island School

I Wish

I wish I did not have such a big head,
I wish I was a popular girl,
I wish all my clothes weren't red,
I wish my hair did not curl.

I wish I did not get the cane,
I wish I was not top of the class,
I wish I did not have all this pain,
I wish I was not so silly in the past.

I wish I had lots of friends,
I wish people would come to my party,
I wish I was locked up in a pen,
I wish I was not a smarty.

Amelia Ward (9)
Mersea Island School

I Wish

I wish I was cool,
I wish I was a skater,
I wish I wasn't a fool,
I wish I was a waiter.

I wish I could be a baker,
I wish I could be a painter,
I wish I wasn't a faker,
I wish I could be a striker.

I wish I had all the time in the world,
I wish I could go wild,
I wish I wasn't filled,
I wish I was skilled.

Harry Rayner (8)
Mersea Island School

I Wish

I wish I had a massive Komodo dragon,
I wish I could be a champion roller skater,
I wish I could meet a phantom,
I wish I had a disintegrator.
I wish that I had all the game cheats,
I wish that my dog Windsor wasn't sick,
I wish I had an army fleet,
I wish I had a stronger kick,
I wish that Dan would pass to me in football,
I wish our dogs wouldn't jump up,
I wish I had a training ball,
I wish our dogs wouldn't throw up.

William May (9)
Mersea Island School

I Wish

I wish most of my games weren't second-hand,
I wish I was simply the best,
I wish my brother went to Neverland,
I wish my dad wasn't a pest.

I wish my brother wasn't a fool,
I wish I had a big rope and a hook,
I wish I had a long pool,
I wish I had a big book.

Sean Ellis (8)
Mersea Island School

I Wish

I wish I was very short,
I wish my hamster could fly up high,
I wish when I played hide-and-seek
I didn't always get caught,
I wish my sister didn't cry.

I wish I was not always taught,
I wish my rabbit didn't die,
I wish I did not have a wart,
I wish I could sprout wings and fly.

Thomas Byrne (9)
Mersea Island School

I Wish

I wish my dog could walk on two legs,
I wish my dad could fly,
I wish my mum wouldn't talk,
I wish nobody would die.

I wish I was big and tough,
I wish I was a mouse,
I wish I was a big, rough person,
I wish I had a bigger house.

I wish I had a nice hat,
I wish I was brave,
I wish I had another kitty cat,
I wish I had a slave!

Amber Ward (8)
Mersea Island School

I Wish

I wish I was cool,
I wish I had a Eurostar,
I wish I wasn't good,
I wish there were more kids.

I wish I was in WWF,
I wish I was fantastic,
I wish I was a good chef,
I wish I was elastic.

I wish I had a raptor,
I wish I was Superman,
I wish I could read a chapter,
I wish I was a man.

Joseph Morehouse (9)
Mersea Island School

I Wish

I wish I could fly in the sky,
I wish there were two of me,
I wish I could always eat pie,
I wish at midnight I could see.

I wish I could vanish in mid-air,
I wish we had more money,
I wish my socks were always in a pair,
I wish my mum was more funny.

I wish I wasn't always bored,
I wish I could have a new globe,
I wish my dad would buy a new Ford,
I wish I could always go to Cudmore Grove.

Thomas Lacy (8)
Mersea Island School

I Wish

I wish Charlotte would stop crying over me,
I wish I was a fighter,
I wish I could unlock the key,
I wish I could fly a kite,
I wish I could fly up to the sky,
I wish I could jump up for joy.

I wish I could dream of a big, juicy pie,
I wish I could be happy,
I wish I had a dragon,
I wish I was a puppy,
I wish I went in a wagon.

Molly Warner-Mattey (9)
Mersea Island School

I Wish

I wish I could fly,
I wish my friends were like me,
I wish I didn't lie,
I wish I didn't have to eat peas,
I wish I didn't blink,
I wish I had everything,
I wish my brain did think,
I wish my bike bell would ring,
I wish you were made of mould,
I wish my clothes were not second-hand,
I wish my house was made out of gold,
I wish I could escape to Neverland.

Charlotte Page (9)
Mersea Island School

I Wish . . .

I wish I had long, golden hair,
I wish I could fly up in the sky,
I wish I had lots more time to spare,
I wish I could cook the biggest apple pie.

I wish I won the World Cup,
I wish I wasn't so chubby,
I wish I didn't look like a dozy duck,
I wish my mum didn't call me 'Bubbles'.

I wish I was rich,
I wish I had a widescreen telly,
I wish I could go on the football pitch,
I wish I could have some jelly.

Rosie Farthing (8)
Mersea Island School

I Wish

I wish I could fly,
I wish I was better at PE,
I wish I could touch the sky,
I wish it was a saltless sea.

I wish I could escape away,
I wish I was better at maths,
I wish I was born on another day,
I wish there were no nasty rats.

I wish my mum didn't buy old clothes,
I wish I had lots more friends,
I wish my family didn't grow,
I wish my mum's glasses didn't have small lenses.

Madeleine Spence (7)
Mersea Island School

The World's Cry

The world's overpowered by war,
Use your voice,
There's cruelty all around us,
Speak your mind,
The animals are suffering testing.
Make a difference,
War is dominating us,
Take action,
Defeat the addiction of drugs and smoking,
Live a full life.
People have no food,
Help them to be healthy.

Elliot Hurry (11)
Mersea Island School

Peace On Earth

Peace on planet Earth,
We explore the future.

Peace on planet Earth,
We care for others.

Peace on planet Earth,
We all work together.

The end of the day,
Peaceful sleep on planet Earth.

Megan Madden (10)
Mersea Island School

Animals

Save animals,
They must not die,
They deserve to live,
Let them see their future,
Let them have babies
To keep going.
Clean the oil and litter
So they will have a happy life too.
They will do the same to you.
Do not experiment on animals,
Let them be free
To run about.
Keep them healthy.
They are kind-hearted,
Give the good-natured animals freedom.
So please defend the animals
To keep them alive, please!

Billy Riley (10)
Mersea Island School

I Wish

I wish my favourite rabbit could sprout out wings and fly,
I wish my clever cat could cook,
I wish I could do one huge leap as high as the sky,
I wish some nice person would do my homework book.

I wish my bedroom would tidy itself,
I wish my climbing frame went on and on for ever and ever,
I wish I could meet an elf,
I wish every day we had nice weather.

Madeline Dyer (9)
Mersea Island School

Australia

Animals in harmony
On the sea and land,
Happiness between families.
The sun shines in the day,
Goes in the night.
The sprinkled sand
Warm in the day,
Peaceful at night.
Helping one another,
Australia, that's the
Place to be.

Amy Markham (10)
Mersea Island School

Save Animals

Save our animals, they don't deserve to die,
They're loving creatures like you and me,
They have feelings too.

So clean all the oil and litter,
Make a happy life for them
And they will do the same for you.

So please, please save the animals.
Please, please, please.

Annie Warner-Mattey (10)
Mersea Island School

A Journey Of Discovery

Fire reflecting on the stars,
An astronaut's smiling face on Mars.
The light of the moon ruling the night,
Won't give it up without a fight.

As quiet as a furry mouse,
As spooky as a dark house,
I wander,
As sandy as the beach,
As slimy as a leech.

As sleepy as the sun,
As busy as my mum,
As cold as a freezer,
As crunchy as a Malteser,
I wait.

Thomas Bonds (10)
Mersea Island School

Space Voyage

We leave planet Earth,
Voyage through space,
Cruising around the world,
Looking back at a piece of Earth.

Shooting past Mars, stars and planets,
Fixing the plates on the dirty shuttle,
Now it is finished.
They travel back to Earth
Remember what it was like in space.

Jonathan Gladwell (11)
Mersea Island School

Space

Space is like a pitch-black field with no one on it.
The sun is like a blazing baseball just been hit.

The stars sparkle like jewels in the dark night.
Mars is like a fireball gazing down on the Earth.

Space is like a dusty room
That has not been cleaned for years.

Joe Scholes (11)
Mersea Island School

Greeks

Dust everywhere,
Soft, like fine hair.
Ancient, crumbly buildings,
Seeing them waiting.
From the old times,
In ancient times, they were mine.

Lara Bird (10)
Mersea Island School

Stars And Planets

Emerging flames from below,
Fire and sparkles as we go,
Look out the window, what do you see?
This is a great experience for me.

Planets and stars as we pass by,
The moon is shining in the night sky.
Jupiter, Mars and Saturn too,
I live on Earth, where do you?

Rosie Storrar-Barfoot (10)
Mersea Island School

Space

I'm having a fit,
I'm slowing my pace,
Fifteen seconds later we will be in space.
We saw the sun,
It's like a piece of sticky chewing gum.
As we passed Mars, we saw elephants in flying cars.
Moonbeams are like thunder that strikes your eye,
If you look too much, you may well die.

Oliver Theobald (11)
Mersea Island School

The Trip

I woke up, I had to be
There in an hour,
When I looked at my lunch
I had cauliflower.
I got on the bus
And with all its power,
We were there
Within two and a half hours.
Sat in a chair with goggles on,
5, 4, 3, 2, 1, lift-off, we were gone.
I stretched my hand out,
I tried to touch the stars.
Wow! I just saw Mars.
I was amazed,
It looked like a big red ball,
What I trip, I was enthralled.

Ben Scholes (11)
Mersea Island School

My Fantasy World

Smoke was like fluffy white candyfloss floating in the sky.
Tension was like toffee, till it's pulled long and high.
Flames were like chilli peppers stuck in your throat,
And the launching of a rocket is the crying of a goat.

The planets were like Smartie balls,
The moon was like white chocolate.
The stars were like big balls of glitter,
And I couldn't see one piece of litter.
Meteors were Maltesers flying way up high,
For we were not on Earth anymore, we were dancing in the sky.

It's time to go back down below,
Where everyone will say hello.
So goodbye moon,
See you soon.
Planets and stars, I'll be back at noon.

Atlanta Whyton (11)
Mersea Island School

My Trip To Space

The planet of power
Was dawned in my mind.
The sound of rockets right behind.
The bright, shaped stars,
Twinkled in the night,
It made my eyes bold and bright.
Rocket shooting up in the air,
I couldn't believe I was actually there.
Now my day is complete,
I can go and have a sleep.

Jessica Blowers (11)
Mersea Island School

A Journey Of Discovery In Space

Space is like a black tablecloth
With large splodges of food on the table,
Mars is a nice helping of tomato ketchup,
Horseradish as the moon,
And a small circular coaster as Pluto.
The small particles of ice like stars from a frozen bag of peas
Just come from the freezer door.
Space was like a feast of wonder,
But now I can enjoy my journey home.

Charlie Fisher (11)
Mersea Island School

Space

I strapped myself in,
Put my suit on,
Ten seconds later,
We were gone.

The sun was shining
Straight in my eye,
I was talking to my friends,
Saying my goodbyes.

Suddenly I was there,
Shocked from the sight,
From the sun comes a ray
Of bright shining light.

Flying past the planets, moon and stars,
A flicker of heat comes from Mars.

Sam Curtis (11)
Mersea Island School

My Trip Out

I couldn't wait to get out of bed
And then my mum called me and said,
'Abbey you are going to be late.'
I was so excited, I couldn't wait.
As I got on the coach,
I strapped myself in
And before I knew it
The wheels started to spin.
Now the coach is on its way,
Our journey has started a brand new day.
I looked out the window and I saw
Trees, cars, lorries and lots more.
We finally arrived and had a great day,
And then we all had to say,
'Thank you very much, it was really good,
I am going to come back, I know I should.'

Abigail Rampton (10)
Mersea Island School

The Planets

T he stars are sparkling in the sky,
H er eyes glow up high.
E arth is so big.

P luto, the planet with a dog,
L ots of planets to see
A fantasy word up here,
N o one can resist it.
E veryone has to come and see
T he time has come, I have to go
S ee you soon in space. I love you so.

Emily Lewis (10)
Mersea Island School

Space

Space is like a black piece of paper,
Sprinkled with silver glitter.
It is like a giant shadow cast over the Earth.
The stars are where small beams of light
Have managed to shine through.
The moon is white and glowing,
Like cream cheese on a dark plate.

Callum Dale (11)
Mersea Island School

Space

Power of a strong hero,
Speed like a mighty race,
Smoke like a rumbling earthquake,
Fire like a spitting bonfire,
Air like a ride in a funfair.

Georgina Davies (11)
Mersea Island School

Space

Planets like big balls of toffee,
The stars that sparkle in the sky,
The moon like a big giant button,
And the rocket that passes by.
The conflagration, flames that fire and spark,
And the rocket that flies off into the dark.

Hannah Willsher (10)
Mersea Island School

Places

Like an antelope we took off,
Faster than Concorde
Speeding up into the air,
Sharper than the sharpest sword.

Giant pillars tower above me,
Amazing statues worn,
Crazy patterns all around me,
Crying for the dawn.

Driving round in little taxis,
The London Eye spins round,
Running round and going places,
Till the night is found.

Samuel Halim (11)
Mersea Island School

I Wish

I wish I could swim the Atlantic Ocean,
I wish I was a funny clown,
I wish I made the world's greatest potion,
I wish I wasn't so down.

I wish my mum didn't buy funny things,
I wish people didn't have to die,
I wish I could be buried in the Valley of the Kings,
I wish my mum would make the best apple pie.

I wish I could have fun all day,
I wish I had a tractor of my own,
I wish people didn't say 'gay',
I wish I wasn't alone.

Jack Trollope (9)
Mersea Island School

A Journey Of Discovery

Fire sparkling in the sky,
The light of the stars as they passed by,
Astronauts circling Mars way up high,
Is my idea of space.

Giant pillars made of stone,
Athene's statue all alone,
Nowhere near the place called home,
Is my idea of Crete.

The hazy glare of the London Eye,
Big Ben's face never to die,
A statue's nose way up high,
Is my idea of London.

Hustle and bustle as far as you can see,
Running around no attention for me,
Flowing as fast as chicken bree,
Is my idea of the Science Museum.

Going home past the trees,
Like an animal as he flees,
Leaving the bus, come and go as you please,
Is my idea of the journey home.

Matthew Whittaker (10)
Mersea Island School

Space

S pace travel
P icture it
A n unexplained world
C ommanding the first ship going into the bleak, unknown chasm
E xtraordinary.

Michael Leyland (10)
Mersea Island School

A Journey In Space

The rage of a dragon,
The energy of a cheetah,
The power of a god,
The thrust of a meteor.
Smoke like a blanket,
Eternity like a maze
And Antares the Supanova
Engulfed in flames.

Thomas Hughes (10)
Mersea Island School

Space

S un like a boiling hot kettle
P assing shooting stars
A star shooting high
C losest neighbour the moon
E normous planets passing by.

Chloe Royce (10)
Mersea Island School

Making A Witch

Take three hairs from a monkey,
Stir them nicely.
Find ten mice and invisible ink,
Find Sam, and take three of his toes,
And then take Charlie's nose.
Now you have to go into Mrs Buckingham's mouth
And pull out her tongue,
And go to the shop to buy some gum.
Give it a final energetic mix,
Then you have the most amazing witch.

Megan Gibbons (11)
Mersea Island School

Man Is Wonderful

Man is wonderful.
He builds great monuments and towers.
But man can be a deadly thing.
Grenades and bombs destroying!
So then the work begins again, builders die of toil,
Now men say, 'No more war, we pray,
And no more awful effort.'
So men hope for war to end as well as pointless labour.

Joshua Richardson (10)
Mersea Island School

Untitled

There was a young girl called Jess
She could be an absolute mess
She loved to wear trousers
For hours and hours
But would never wear a long dress.

Nicolle Dickson (9)
Mersea Island School

Scary Mary

Scary Mary is a horrible witch,
Sometimes she gets an itch,
She scratches and catches her maggoty nails,
She tries not to bite them but miserably fails,
Did you know she eats snails?
How do you know Scary Mary's a witch?
Because she has an itch.
Scary Mary's a whispering witch.

Jayne Christie (10)
R A Butler Junior School

Horses

Horses galloping along on sand and in grass
With their manes flowing behind them
In the bright day sky,
Their shiny bay coats glistening in the afternoon sun,
Their delicate hooves gently hitting the ground
As the horses gallop along.

If I had a horse my lifetime dream would come true,
I would never be alone and would always have a friend.
I would call it Baloo, or maybe Shadow, I think,
But whatever I do, I'll always love horses,
They are the *best animals in the world!*

Lizzie Clark (9)
R A Butler Junior School

Snowdrift

Snow glittering in the sunlight,
Snow soft as cream.
Snow, powdery as icing sugar,
Snow makes me dream.
Snow shines crystal clear.

Ice crunching beneath my feet,
Ice crackling like 2D fireworks,
Ice crumbling on the pond,
Ice reflecting on the snowy mound,
Ice slippery and smooth.

Snowballs in the air,
Cars skidding on the road,
House rooftops wearing a new coat of white,
Children building merry snowmen,
Common covered in a white sheet of snow.

Andrew Breed (11)
R A Butler Junior School

Dogs

(Inspired by 'Cats Sleep Anywhere' by Eleanor Farjeon)

Dogs sleep anywhere, any table, any chair,
They will play with any ball,
And won't listen to the rule.
Even though they eat meat,
They are very sweet.
Whatever you do, don't leave your food on the side,
Or *munch, munch, munch!*

Jasmine Barker (9)
R A Butler Junior School

Food!

Chocolate bar,
Strawberry milkshake,
Victoria sponge,
Chocolate cake.

Chicken, pizza,
(All you can eatser),
with a fast food lunch,
(What a munch).

Everything
Sweets to meat,
Fast food recipes
And I'll eat all I can eat!

But semolina pudding
And vegetable muck,
This is what I'm given,
All my luck!

Alice Marks (9)
R A Butler Junior School

If I Wasn't Me, What Would I Be?

Perhaps I'd be a cheetah!
To be the fastest creature.
My speckled coat of shiny gold
Would make me feel so brave and bold.

Or perhaps I'd be a bat!
Yes I'd quite fancy that.
I could spread my wings
And see with my great eyes a thousand things.

Maybe I'd be a fish!
All scaly, oh I wish.
I'd breathe through my gills
To show my frills.

Still I like being me!
I could still dream these things,
But, will it be much fun?

Edward Pottrill (9)
R A Butler Junior School

My Day Out!

Out we go,
Far and wide,
Travelling quick,
Fast with pride,
Going to Cadbury's
For some fun,
Now eating chocolate,
At least a ton!

Maisie Walker (10)
R A Butler Junior School

My Box

(Based on 'Magic Box' by Kit Wright)

I shall put in my box . . .
Some wind from the great storm of 1986,
Some mist from the middle of the Pacific Ocean,
A spell from the great wizard Merlin.

I shall put in my box . . .
The roar of an angry lion that hasn't eaten for days,
The leaf of a plant at the top of Mont Blanc,
The first word ever spoken by a human.

My box is fashioned from . . .
Wood from a boat, sunk in the Atlantic Ocean,
The petal of a rare, extinct flower,
Sapphires from the middle of the Earth.

I shall dream in my box
And not forget anything that I have put in it.
I shall dream in my box.

Philip Jones (11)
R A Butler Junior School

Tiger's Eye

Tiger's Eye is a type of quartz,
It may come out in different sorts,

But it might not be what you think,
And no, it isn't pink.

It may be a fossilized eye,
That rolls out when tigers die.

But just remember, Tiger's Eye is a type of quartz,
It may come out in different sorts.

Orla McCormick (11)
R A Butler Junior School

Shadow

The shadow races up the field,
And lands in not a shadow,
With a gallant sigh
He walks on by,
Past the dark grey shadow.

The shadow is nearly there,
He wants to stop and rest,
I see now, I know now,
That I will win the race.

The shadow wins the race to the field
And receives the great, grand prize.
He slowly turns back
Without the sight of the other great, grand shadow.

Molly Adams (10)
R A Butler Junior School

Games

There is hopscotch
Or maybe croquet,
Boys like football
And girls like ballet.

I like the hurdles,
You may like to sprint,
I like high jump
And others like to swim.

Golf is great, I like to
Hit the ball straight,
Basketball is fun if
You like to run.

Sport is good for one and all,
It improves your skills
And can stop you from being ill.

Hannah Parker (10)
R A Butler Junior School

Get You

He drew a monster
On the inside cover
Of his library book.
That was at bedtime,
But he fell asleep.

By morning
His monster
Seemed bigger,
Its eyes
More open wide.
Its ears more pointed,
A drop of blood
Flecked its chin.

By bedtime
That night
It was itching
Towards the edge of the paper.
As he quickly closed the book,
The monster grinned.

Thomas Ash (10)
R A Butler Junior School

The Beautiful Game

The crowd is roaring from the south-west stand,
The national anthem comes from the band,
The players come out
Without any doubt
That they will win the final,
That they will win the final.

The players look smart,
And now they start,
England v Brazil,
But at full-time it's still nil-nil,
Can they win the final?
Can they win the final?

Then Rooney nets the golden goal,
And the England flag goes up on a pole,
They have won the cup,
Oh, what skill, what luck,
They have won the final.
They have won the final!

Rafi Hilali (10)
R A Butler Junior School

Holiday Poem

Canoeing with the whales,
Faster and faster they go,
Pat them,
Feed them
And even jump on them.

Galloping through the mountains
With your brown and black horse,
Past the rivers,
Through the waterfalls,
Jump over rocks,
Land on the stones,
Crunch, crunch, crunch.

Hike up the Rockies,
Past the deadly rocks,
Up and up I go,
Faster and faster.
Nearly made it,
I'm nearly there,
Yes, yes,
I'm finally here.

Jessica Hargrave (9)
R A Butler Junior School

The Colour Collector

(Based on 'The Sound Collector' by Roger McGough)

A stranger called this morning
Dressed in black and grey,
Put every colour into a bag
And carried them all away.

The yellow of the sun,
The blue of the sky,
The silver of the diamonds
Glistening in my eye.

The purple of my bedroom,
The orange of the fire,
The red of the roses,
That's my heart's desire.

The pink of the late night sunset,
The brown of the trunk of the tree,
The green of the leaves as they lay on the floor,
The gold of the shining tea.

A stranger called this morning,
He didn't leave his name,
Left us no colour,
Life will never be the same.

Rachel Procter (11)
R A Butler Junior School

The Magic Box

(Based on 'Magic Box' by Kit Wright)

I will put in the box . . .
Haiku spells, invisible ink, stardust from the sky above,
Curses from Tutankhamen's tomb,
A skull from the dead.

I will put in the box . . .
A halo from an angel,
A prong from Neptune's triton,
The Devil's flame.

I will put in the box . . .
The first ever flower born on Earth,
The source of a river,
The seed of an exotic palm tree.

I will put in the box . . .
The power of invisibility,
A man's last breath,
A baby's first smile.

My box is fashioned from
Pure, fiery gold,
Crystals from Pluto,
The silkworm's finest silk
And the hinges are the woolly mammoth's toe joints.

I shall rule my country in my box,
I shall build the world's highest building within it,
And then I shall hide my box
For someone else to find it.

Oliver Sandles (11)
R A Butler Junior School

My Box

(Based on 'Magic Box' by Kit Wright)

I will put in my box . . .
Deep down, dark secrets,
With memories of my loved ones who have died.

I will put in my box . . .
The source of all my fears,
The touch of a dolphin's tooth,
And leopard's skin.

My box is fashioned from
Bottle-nosed dolphin's skin,
Spirals on it like curled up hedgehogs,
And the softness of a baby's bottom.

I shall swim with great blue whales
And swing with talking monkeys
In the middle of the Caribbean,
And never return!

Lauren King (10)
R A Butler Junior School

Chocolate

Chocolate, chocolate, creamy chocolate,
It sits on the tip of my tongue.
Chocolate, chocolate, yummy chocolate,
Slips off my tongue into my tum.
Chocolate, chocolate, luscious chocolate,
It's just as nice as Mum, so give her some!

Elizabeth Murphy (9)
R A Butler Junior School

My Box

(Based on 'Magic Box' by Kit Wright)

I will put in the box . . .
A diamond forged in the centre of the Earth,
The first of God's creations,
Fire from the largest dragon.

I will put in the box . . .
An extract from Jupiter's spot,
Justice and democracy,
A pet Siberian tiger.

My box is fashioned from the gold of Rameses' tomb,
Russian war diamonds, stardust,
And the lock is a riddle,
The answer, only I know.

I shall rule supreme in my box.
I shall build my own civilization,
Then I will command it.

James Mackintosh (11)
R A Butler Junior School

The Caribbean

The Caribbean,
lots of soft, powdery sand
under the palm trees.
The clear, blue, salty water,
little waves rippling along.

Lucy Sumner (10)
R A Butler Junior School

My Box . . .

(Based on 'Magic Box' by Kit Wright)

I will put in my box . . .
A wing of an angel with a tear full of hope,
A flame from evil as dark as night,
A plate of gold from the finest block of earth.

I will put in my box . . .
Imagination with a rainbow, colourful like truth,
Memories powerful, like a swoop from a hawk,
And a smile from each corner of the earth.

My box is fashioned from . . .
Delicate white silk,
With thread of rich black velvet,
With fragile gems, precious as life itself.

I shall visit places in my box,
Like to the furthest star in space,
Then capture it and treasure it in my box.

Zoë Camp (11)
R A Butler Junior School

Poppy

I lay every day under the ground,
I stay here all fixed, never to be found.
My body is gone but I might get a chance
To come out and see light with one glance.

My siblings are gone but they're left alone,
To lie there and listen to the silent tone.
Why, oh why does this happen so much?
I cry and cry, then with a little touch,
I grow and the sunlight hits me,
My stem gets longer and I just start to see
How beautiful I can be.

My petals fall off, but my seed life's not bad,
And I grow again . . . and again . . . and again.

Tilly Sleven (10)
R A Butler Junior School

My Box

(Based on 'Magic Box' by Kit Wright)

I will put in my box . . .
The whole wide world,
The crust of the Earth
And a shooting star, taking me for a ride.

I will put in my box . . .
A hair from a caveman, my prehistoric relative,
A tooth from the future,
An empty space.

I will put in my box . . .
The day of my birthday,
A great big smile
And a family get together.

I will put in my box . . .
My thoughts and memories,
A stadium for any sport,
A teddy I've had since a baby.

My box is fashioned from Antarctica,
Made from ice that will never melt
And sprinkled with sequins from India.

In the box I will . . .
Visit America, France, Spain and Japan,
I will play in the sea and walk up mountains,
Then I'll visit the moon.

Lauren Coates (11)
R A Butler Junior School

Little Angel

Now let's start from the beginning,
By the lighthouse rocks,
A tortured girl was driven here
Through bullies' painful mocks.

I'll take you back a month ago
To see just what took place,
Explore her mournful cry of help
And tears left on her face.

Going back just two months more
Let's see how things went wrong,
You'll see she's calm as calm could be,
But this will not last long.

Bullies come in quite large groups
And this gang was the same,
They blacked and bruised her body
But they saw it as a game.

She did not speak all day long,
Not a single note,
Getting home she found a pen
And this is what she wrote:

'I do not blame the bullies,
My heart still holds some love,
I'm still your little angel,
Just watching from above'.

Patience Foster (10)
R A Butler Junior School

My Box

(Based on 'Magic Box' by Kit Wright)

I will put in the box . . .
The day that England won the cup,
The second that Jonny Wilkinson's boot
Touched the winning ball,
A kick-flip down a case of stairs.

I will put in the box . . .
When it snowed in the middle of June,
The sensation of being picked for the team,
The first bit of chocolate ever made.

My box is fashioned from
A bit of wood, shaped as a skateboard,
With diamonds from Jupiter,
So bright that civilisation can't look at it.
The wood is from the local tree of South Africa.
The inside is covered in ostrich feathers.

Alfie Smith (10)
R A Butler Junior School

My Bedroom

In my bedroom I will keep . . .
My pet dragon,
The sunniest beach,
And my mum's home cooking.

In my bedroom I will keep . . .
The highest tidal wave,
The flash of a lightning bolt,
And the brain of Frankenstein.

My bedroom has blue wallpaper,
The door handle is a king's skull,
My cupboard takes you to Narnia,
And my teddy is made from the hair of a stone.

Daniel Mills (10)
R A Butler Junior School

My Kitten

My kitten may look scary
With her sharp and yellow teeth,
But if she gets annoyed,
She will pounce and eat your feet.

My kitten may looked scary
With her sharp and yellow teeth,
But if she gets annoyed,
Just let her have some meat.

My kitten may look scary
With her sharp and yellow teeth,
But if she gets afraid,
She will run to have something to eat.

My kitten may look scary
With her sharp and yellow teeth,
But really, she's as soft as anything
And I can't help thinking she is so sweet.

My kitten may look scary
With her sharp and yellow teeth,
But when I come home from school
She's always there to greet.

My kitten may look scary
With her sharp and yellow teeth,
She'll place herself on me,
Then go and find another seat.

My kitten may look scary
With her sharp and yellow teeth,
And as she looks so dirty,
She is also very neat.

When I think of her,
I just want to give her a treat!

Hannah Monk (9)
R A Butler Junior School

Christmas Luck!

The
Angel falls
Backward off
The tall tree. Mary
Drops Jesus at the
Nativity. Santa gets stuck,
Stuck fast in next-door's chimney.
Ten pairs of socks are given to me.
For Christmas lunch,
I got the burnt bit of turkey.
The Christmas pudding when
Set alight burnt me. Something got
Thrown at me, possibly a pea. The dog
Went around licking everyone's knees, the
Baby cried when
Grandma started to
Sneeze, at least this Christmas
Was better than last year!

Harriet Evans (11)
R A Butler Junior School

My Box

(Based on 'Magic Box' by Kit Wright)

I will put in my box . . .
World War Three,
The horn of a Minotaur,
The head of a fox.

I will put in my box . . .
A necron from a distant world,
A giant flayer ray gun,
And blood from a Martian.

My box is fashioned from a rock from Mars,
The hinges are gas from an unknown star,
The handle is the leg of a cursed chicken.

I shall treasure my box,
Visit extraordinary worlds with it,
Then pass it down through my life,
But I will never open it.

Thomas Horrigan (10)
R A Butler Junior School

Chocolate

Chocolate is so delicious and tempting.
It is always there, there in front of me.

It is always on my mind,
Chocolate, chocolate, chocolate.
Dark chocolate, light chocolate,
It's all the same.

I have a little bite, well maybe a couple.
It is there in front of me.
I have another bite; well no one else is going to eat it!

That was *delicious.*

Jessica Quinn (10)
St Margaret's CE Primary School, Halstead

The Jungle

Animals, animals are all the same,
Some of them are even in a game.
Rumble in the jungle, Scrabble too
God who made animals for me and you.
If you want a wicked time,
Then come down to the jungle,
Where we can all rhyme.

Lauren Platt (8)
St Margaret's CE Primary School, Halstead

Look At Me!

Look at me, I'm a bee
Look at me, I can see!
Look at me, I drink tea!
Look at me, I can be free!
But why can't I find the key?

Alexander Barnes (8)
St Margaret's CE Primary School, Halstead

The Man

The wind was howling, it was cold,
A man came walking, very brave and bold.

He had a stick and he had a pipe,
He had a pear that was ripe.

The floor was covered like a white sheet
That nibbled at his bare feet.

Suzanna Michael (10)
St Margaret's CE Primary School, Halstead

Post

Post is good. Post is bad.
When it's late it makes you mad.
To our door the postman nears,
The dog has just pricked up his ears.
He takes the letters out of his bag
And puts them in the letter box.
The dog shoots out and bites his socks.
The postman had a heavy bag;
He dropped it on the floor and ran.
On his bike he gets
And off he goes with a sweat.

Molly-May Stevenson (7)
St Margaret's CE Primary School, Halstead

Christmas

Christmas, Christmas all the same,
Presents downstairs, it's only a game.
Come on, come on, let's have some fun,
Because the day has just begun.

Santa is coming, but he is running,
Santa is late because he has just opened the gate!
Santa is ill because he has the chill.

Christmas, Christmas all the same,
Presents downstairs, it's only a game.
Come on, come on, let's have some fun,
Because the day has just begun.

George Quinn (8)
St Margaret's CE Primary School, Halstead

Dogs

Dogs bark in the day,
Dogs bark in the night,
Dogs love to play,
Dogs love to fight.

Dogs hate being left in,
Dogs hate being left alone,
Dogs love food from the tin,
Dogs love a nice, juicy bone.

Dogs love it in the summer,
Dogs hate it in the cold,
Dogs like it when it's funner,
Dogs like being bold.

Dogs bark in the day,
Dogs bark in the night,
Dogs love to play,
Dogs love to fight.

Connie James (9)
St Margaret's CE Primary School, Halstead

Fearsome . . .

Fearsome, fearsome Labrador,
Can you close that draughty door?
It's been creaking all night long,
Can you sing your funny song?
Fearsome, fearsome Labrador,
Can you close that draughty door?

James Mortlock (8)
St Margaret's CE Primary School, Halstead

The Fish And The Labrador

(Based on 'The Owl And The Pussy-Cat' by Edward Lear)

The fish and the Labrador
Went on tour
In an ugly old brown wooden ship,
They took some lollies and plenty of dollies,
Screwed up in a coat with a zip!

The fish looked down to the sea below
And said to the Labrador,
'Oh sweet little puppy, oh puppy my sweet,
What a pretty young puppy you are!
You are, you are,
What a pretty young puppy you are.'
Puppy said to the fish, 'You cook a nice dish
And what lovely words you say!
Why let us be carried; too long we've *just* been married,
But what shall we do for a lift?'

They floated away for a month and a day,
To the place where the ping-wood grows;
And there in the forest a duck stood,
With muscles as big as a huge boat!
Huge boat, huge boat,
With muscles as big as a huge boat!

So they were carried away and danced the next day,
With the tall, strong duck with huge muscles,
They ate food with a cat in a mood,
Which they killed with a gold knife and fork;

Then hand in hand, they kissed by the soft sand,
And swam in the very deep sea,
Deep sea, deep sea,
And swam in the very deep sea.

Hannah Pyman (9)
St Margaret's CE Primary School, Halstead

The Waterfall

The waterfall flows loudly and fast
As you sit there peacefully the water gently goes past.
As you look over little stones, pebbles and things appear,
Then they softly disappear.
The tiny creatures swim and hide,
As they slowly pass your side.
Animals come to drink at the waterfall,
Many of them are very tall.
All the animals went away,
I was left there for the rest of the day.

Erika Chinery (10)
St Margaret's CE Primary School, Halstead

Easter

Today I'm going out shopping to buy my Easter egg,
I'm going with my best friend Meg.
I love Easter eggs, I have five every year,
And I'm going to the shop which is near.
I'm looking forward to seeing the Easter Bunny,
Sometimes he even gives me money.
At Easter time it is spring,
I hear the birds in my garden sing
At Easter time when the flowers come out,
It is fun when I run about.
As well as an Easter egg, I have a hot cross bun.
Easter is so much fun!

Amelia Quinn (9)
St Margaret's CE Primary School, Halstead

Alphabet Of Kids' Characteristics

A is for April who likes cats,
B is for Ben who slips on mats,
C is for Colin who picks his nose,
D is for Danielle who stubs her toes,
E is for Emily who likes to drink water,
F is for Fredina who is the queen's daughter,
G is for Georgina who keeps strange pets,
H is for Horace who fishes with nets,
I is for Ione who lives on a farm,
J is for Jack who has a long arm,
K is for Kathy who has peacocks,
L is for Laura who has lots of socks,
M is for Max who is a clown,
N is for Nick whose trousers fall down,
O is for Oliver who wears a vest,
P is for Pippa who always tries her best,
Q is for Quinton who loves parties,
R is for Richard who eats lots of Smarties,
S is for Sam who loves books,
T is for Tina who has good looks,
U is for Ursula who hates her name,
V is for Violet who is all the same,
W is for Wayne who is silly,
X is for Xerxes who is really called Billy,
Y is for Yasmin who is very posh,
Z is for Zak who has loads of dosh!

Emily Skipp (9)
St Peter's CE Primary School, Sible Hedingham

Teachers

Teachers are so strict,
They think they are the boss.
They always make us work
And learn lots of stuff.
Even if we beg, they won't let us play,
They won't let us play, play, play all day.
They overload us with homework,
There's really strict detention, 100 lines and more.
I don't know why we can't play,
Because they lounge around all day,
Drinking cups of coffee.

Rosie Ranson (9)
St Peter's CE Primary School, Sible Hedingham

Bonfire

Bonfire crackling, fireworks up high,
New ones whistling in the sky.
Rockets are racing like I've never seen before,
So keep your animals in and lock the door.
Catherine wheels are twirling, sparks are flying off,
The dog is going mad and deafening me with a woof.
Fireworks are great, nice and red,
But keep waking me up when I'm in bed.
But apart from that I must say,
'Happy Guy Fawkes day.'

Jordan Wheeler (9)
St Peter's CE Primary School, Sible Hedingham

Little Liar

Little liar Tommy Grain
Chucked some froggies down the drain,
He blamed it on Georgina Doss,
His teacher, Cressley, was very cross.
She started to cry,
She was very shy,
She told him it was Tommy Grain,
She wouldn't chuck froggies down the drain.
Her teacher, Cressley slid away,
Hoping to sort this mess out some way,
Wishing that he could give detention
And also to be in the next dimension.
Tommy Grain would not give up,
This time he blamed it on Sam Cup
And this time Cressley was not a fool,
He dumped Tommy in the swimming pool.
Tommy Grain drowned away,
Hooray for Mr Edward Cressley.

Danielle Rainer (8)
St Peter's CE Primary School, Sible Hedingham

Joy

Joy is a day full of glee,
Joy is a day for you and me.
Joy can make me sing a song,
Joy can make me smile all day long.

Laura Nunn (9)
St Peter's CE Primary School, Sible Hedingham

What Am I?

Funny walker,
Strange waddler,
Non-flyer,
Strong swimmer,
Sea glider,
Great diver,
Egg layer,
Fish muncher,
Baby carrier,
Ice stalker,
Water drinker,
Short legger,
Antarctic liver,
Fantastic flapper,
Food hunter,
Hopeless flyer,
Small beaker,
Hill slider.

What am I?

A penguin.

Karena Suckling (10)
St Peter's CE Primary School, Sible Hedingham

Autumn Days

A pples ripe and ready to be eaten,
U p, up in the tree the conkers are starting to fall,
T he trees are losing their leaves,
U nder the ground the nuts are buried.
M y feet crush the leaves as I walk,
N ow it's harvest time, hip, hip, hooray.

Hannah Joy (9)
St Peter's CE Primary School, Sible Hedingham

What Am I?

Fish eater,
Clam beater,
Head bobber,
Beak slobberer,
Pouch storer,
Strong diver,
Funny flapper,
Bucket beaker,
Loud screecher,
Water drinker,
Lake glider,
Egg layer,
Brilliant flyer,
Slow walker,
Water lover.

What am I?

A pelican.

Christie Sharp (10)
St Peter's CE Primary School, Sible Hedingham

Summer

S ummer is fun with glee
U nder the leaves and crawl
M uttering in the crowd is fun in the sun
M unching berries from the trees
E very day is a beautiful day
R espect for your family is nice with trust.

Kimberley Whitehouse (9)
St Peter's CE Primary School, Sible Hedingham

Food

No one wants to eat me,
Because I'm a fish in a tank.
Just because I was in the deep blue sea,
People think I taste *blank!*

No one wants to eat me too,
It's just not fair.
I'm only a chicken, what did I do?
Did I peck at someone they liked?

No one wants to eat me either,
I'm only a lamb.
They put me on a barbecue!
But then replaced me with some ham.

Laurie Hunter (9)
St Peter's CE Primary School, Sible Hedingham

Summer

Daisies in the meadow
Blowing in the breeze.
Children in the playground
Playing with a ball.

A little black cat
Climbing up the wall.
Birds up above
Singing in the trees.

Rowan Hood (9)
St Peter's CE Primary School, Sible Hedingham

What Am I?

Swinging gobbler,
Corn stuffer,
Brother impersonator,
Vein glower,
Finger biter,
Nose nipper,
Sharp beaker,
A horrid bother,
Feather shower,
Fast runner,
Body wrinkler,
Children scarer,
Egg layer,
Bad looker,
Grass liker,
Cat hater,
Human annoyer,
Odd colour,
Nonsense talker,
Sharp nailer,
Christmas dinner!

What am I?

A turkey!

Natisha Chatten (10)
St Peter's CE Primary School, Sible Hedingham

The Cat

The cat sat on the mat,
Wearing a hat.
He wanted a pet bat,
But he couldn't have that,
So he got a pet rat.

Harlie Cornish (10)
St Peter's CE Primary School, Sible Hedingham

The River

The river is skin bumping gracefully over bones.
It is blue icing spread over a chocolate cake.
It is a road, the traffic moving steadily.
It is a bulldozer eating away at rock.
It is a sparkler spraying its sparks.
It is a person growing from a baby into an adult.

Gracia Moss (10)
Stanway Primary School

Frost Haiku

Go Mr Tom Snow
Whiten all your freezing mist
Paint the world for us.

Adam Rhaiti (7)
Stanway Primary School

A Waterfall

A waterfall is a bomb of blue tiles
Crashing on rocks as they fall down.
It is raging adults, falling, falling,
Shouting and shouting.
A plunge pool is frothing lemon,
Whirling around as the adults and tiles fall.
A waterfall is a place where the tiles and adults
Fall further and further.

Emily Dowrick (10)
Stanway Primary School

What Is A River?

A river is a class full of blue jumpers
All cramped together.
It is a car's motor going along the street.
It is the softness of a rug
Just come home from the shop.
It is a cloth newly washed on a summer's day
In a field of flowers.
It is a taste of vinegar splashed over my dinner.

Sacha Sibley (9)
Stanway Primary School

What Is The River?

The river is a conveyor belt
That's gone haywire.

It's a Trojan ram
Bashing against you.

It's an army of Greek soldiers
Charging at myth units.

It's a giant blast of fresh air.

It's a hungry blue monster
Trying to eat stones.

Jonathan Lam (9)
Stanway Primary School

Grandad's Gone

No more sitting on Grandad's knee,
No more paddling with him in the sea.
Why does this happen to me?

No more running past his chair,
No more going to the fair.
Why does this have to be?

No more reading me a bedtime book,
No more getting tickled on my foot.
Why does he have to leave me?

No more jumping on his bed,
No more snuggling in his bed.
Nothing like this should be.

No more time to sing this song,
Going, going, going, gone.

Ellen Horwood & Matilda Young (10)
Stanway Primary School

What Is A River?

The river is a bottle of water
Spilling over a table.

The river is water falling off the table onto the floor,
Like a waterfall into a plunge pool.

It is a long strip of ribbon, curling and twisting,
And when it hits the rocks it splits,
Like the scissors cutting it.

It is a Ferrari speeding up the motorway.

Christian Stephens (9)
Stanway Primary School

The Snow

The snow is bitter cold,
Like a running waterfall in North America.
Very cold,
Like a car splashing through a puddle.
Very fruitless,
Like a loud plane landing on a wet runway.
Smells like a mashed banana.
Faded like a hard rock hitting your face,
Freezing like you have just been stung.
Is like a smiley face.
It glistens like a beautiful bird.
It shines, like the trophy from the World Cup.

Joshua Wren (8)
Stanway Primary School

What Is A River?

The river is a long blue sheet
Sailing in the sky.

It is a tap
That has been left on.

It's a smooth silk
Patchwork quilt.

It is a field of flowers.
It tastes like mouthwash.

Sam Pelosi (10)
Stanway Primary School

What Is A River?

The river is a car
Speeding down the motorway.

It is a long blue sheet,
Deep, deep down in a green quilt.

It is a blue jumper,
Just washed.

It is a herd of animals
Crashing against the boundary of a tree.

It is a blue silk ribbon
Put around a green iced cake.

Chloe Veal (9)
Stanway Primary School

What Is A River?

The river is a rattle
Shaking in the blue sky.

It is a child splashing in puddles
As it rains.

It is a bunch of flowers
Waiting to be bought.

It is a tap dripping
Into a huge bath.

It is smooth silk
That's just been washed.

Kerry Foy (10)
Stanway Primary School

The Snow

The snow is freezing like a frozen freezer in your house.
The snow is depressed like a man
Who just lost his wife in a car crash.
The snow is dismal like a rainy day at school
The snow is happy like a school of
Happy fish in a pond.
The snow is delighted like a boy on his birthday.
The snow is rank like a dead chicken.

Dominic Harris (9)
Stanway Primary School

The Young River

The water plunges down into a hundred metre deep bath,
It then uses its teeth to cut through a muddy, thick ribbon,
While the other beam finds its own way.
Then they meet up like they have known each other for years
And become a hyper beam.
Then it starts to crash and bash against the rocks,
And then, and then, and then!
It dies down and floats away to the sea.

Sam Clayton (10)
Stanway Primary School

The River

It is a never-ending, uncoiling piece of rope,
It is busting and rusting everything in its way.
It does the same every day,
It braids up into several channels.
It is a spy,
It is an army charging, never to be beaten,
It is their spears that spray the land,
It is an undiscovered land deep down.

Joseph Raynor (10)
Stanway Primary School

Waterfall

Waterfall, waterfall,
What are you . . . ?

You are a slippery slide
Steep and strong,

You are a blue ribbon,
Racing and running,

You are a parachute,
Up, down, up, down,

You are a bunch of blue flowers,
Down
    Down,
        Splash,
Whirlpool whizzing like
A jacuzzi.

Hannah Webdale (10)
Stanway Primary School

The River

The river is a roaring beast
Attacking its prey.
It is an immortal army
Relentlessly attacking a castle.
It is a Formula 1 racing car
Zooming round the corners of the track.
It is a boomerang, twisting and turning
And doubling back on itself.
It is a child muttering to an adult.

Ryan Mead (10)
Stanway Primary School